GLOUCESTER
MURDER
& CRIME

GLOUCESTER
MURDER
& CRIME

JILL EVANS

The
History
Press

First published 2013

The History Press
The Mill, Brimscombe Port
Stroud, Gloucestershire, GL5 2QG
www.thehistorypress.co.uk

British Library Cataloguing in Publication Data.
A catalogue record for this book is available from the British Library.

ISBN 978 0 7524 6750 4

Typesetting and origination by The History Press
Printed in Great Britain

CONTENTS

INTRODUCTION

Gloucester in the late nineteenth and early twentieth centuries had several important roles: as a cathedral city; as a municipal borough; as the county town of Gloucestershire; and as an inland port. In contemporary guides, Gloucester was depicted as a peaceful place, dominated by the cathedral and full of quaint buildings, such as the ancient New Inn. In reality, of course, the city saw its fair share of disorder and crime, illustrated in the newspaper reports of the petty sessions, which saw a daily procession of miscreants accused of drunkenness, violence and thieving.

It is, then, surprising to discover that in the nineteenth and early twentieth centuries, when compared to the county as a whole, the city and borough of Gloucester suffered relatively little serious crime. As the county town, the assizes for the county and the city were held at Gloucester, and while the eminent judges who presided at them often berated the county magistrates over the large number of cases brought to trial, those of the city paradoxically were praised for the small number of felons on their calendars.

The most serious crime any human being could commit was, of course, murder. Between 1872 and 1939, seventeen people were hanged for murder at Gloucester Prison, but only one of them committed their crime in the city. This did not mean that no one in Gloucester was tried on a charge of murder, but juries by the second half of the nineteenth century were reluctant to condemn a prisoner to death, and wherever possible looked for mitigating circumstances which allowed a sentence to be reduced to one of manslaughter. There were also, of course, times when the bodies of apparent murder victims were found, but the person who committed the crime was never discovered.

This volume looks at some of the most interesting cases of murder, attempted murder and manslaughter which took place in Gloucester between 1873 and 1934. Several of Gloucester's institutions feature in these stories, including the infirmary, the County Gaol, the courthouses at the back of Shire Hall and, in two cases, the County Lunatic Asylum, which

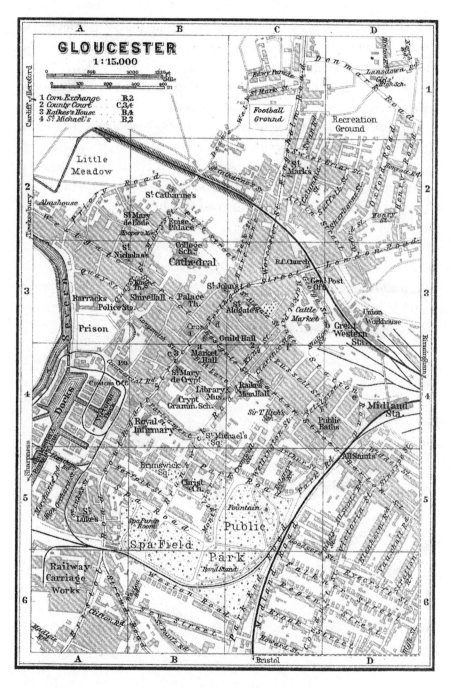

Map of Gloucester in 1910, published by Baedeker. (Author's collection)

played an important role in two of the cases. In one, the death of an inmate who was found to have unexplained injures caused such an outcry that the Home Secretary became involved. In the other, the discharge of a patient as 'cured' led to tragic consequences for one Gloucester family. One case concerned foreign sailors involved in a fracas outside a Gloucester public house; in another, the scene of the crime was the Gloucester and Berkeley Canal. The rest took place in terraced houses, overheard by neighbours through paper-thin walls, in streets where everyone knew everyone else's business, and where it was noticed if a member of the community went missing.

Researching the true stories which are told in this volume was helped greatly by the contemporary reports on inquests, remand hearings and trials, which were recorded in great detail in Gloucester's local newspapers, in particular *The Citizen* and the *Gloucester Journal*.

Grateful thanks are offered to Gloucestershire Archives for giving permission to reproduce images from their newspaper holding and illustrations from other items in their collections.

Jill Evans, 2013

'THEY'RE KILLING ME!'

Suspect:	Otto Moritz
Age:	Unknown
Charge:	Murder

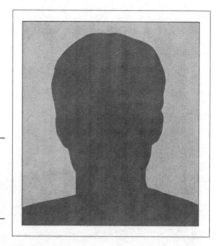

Strangers coming to Gloucester in Victorian times would probably have been surprised to find that the atmosphere was more like that of a port than of an inland city. One such visitor was the writer and art historian Mrs Schuyler Van Rensselaer, who wrote in *The Century* magazine that on coming into the city she saw masts and sails, and described how great vessels came up the River Severn to Gloucester, 'and lay in its capacious pools almost beneath the shadow of the cathedral tower. Here one may find sailors in the streets, smell tar, and fancy one smells salt; yet a pastoral country lies all around.'

Gloucester had held the status of a port since 1580, by virtue of a grant made by Queen Elizabeth I, but began to flourish when the Gloucester and Berkeley Canal opened in 1827, allowing seagoing vessels to bypass the difficult stretch of water on the approach into the city. The Gloucester and Berkeley Canal (later renamed the Gloucester and Sharpness) proved to be a great success, and brought in barges, trows and sailing ships carrying cargoes of timber, corn and wine from Ireland, continental Europe, Russia and North America.

In February 1873, a German brig named the *Gustav* arrived at the docks, carrying a cargo of timber from Dantzic, North Germany (now Gdansk in Poland). One of the crew was a ship's carpenter named Otto Moritz, who was a native of Dantzic. He took lodgings at the Barley Mow inn near to the docks. This was a small establishment, situated in Southgate Street, opposite the County Infirmary. The landlady, Ann Jones, was a widow who had taken over running the pub after her husband died.

Sketch of Gloucester Docks in *The Century* magazine, 1890. (Author's collection)

Engraving of Gloucester Docks by M. Mossman, 1842. (Author's collection)

On Monday, 3 March, a French barque named *Bayonnaise* came into Gloucester docks. Four sailors on board – Emanuel Evain, Emile Poirrier, Etienne Mayon and Joseph Machevaux – left the boat that evening and went into Gloucester together. After spending the evening drinking at various establishments, they made their way down Southgate Street towards the docks at a few minutes before eleven o'clock. As they passed the Barley Mow, they saw that the door was still open, and so they went in. Ann Jones served the French sailors a quart of beer, but asked them to drink up quickly, as it was nearly closing time. The men, however, did not hurry, and Mrs Jones poured away some of their beer. They then got up to leave, but as they did so, Mrs Jones gave a shriek and said she had been hit in the eye by one of the four Frenchmen.

Otto Moritz followed the men outside and attacked two of them with a knife. One of them was Emanuel Evain, who ran towards the docks, clutching his thigh. The other was Emile Poirrier, who was kicked and stabbed by Moritz

'kicked and stabbed'

as he lay on the ground. Witnesses fetched the police, and Poirrier was soon taken to hospital. Evain, though, was not found until later, near the dock gates, and after being taken to the infirmary, he died.

Otto Mortiz was quickly identified as the man who had attacked the two sailors, and he was arrested. On Wednesday, 5 March, he appeared at the City Police Court before the mayor and other magistrates, charged with the murder of Emanuel Evain. The court was very crowded, as there was a great deal of interest in the case among the local population. French and German interpreters were present to help translate the evidence. Mr Taynton, for the prosecution, gave a summary of the events of 3 March, and then called witnesses, whose testimony revealed the details of what had happened two nights before.

The first to give his evidence was one of the French sailors, Etienne Mayon, who, through his interpreter, said that he was a seaman on board the *Bayonnaise*, and that Emanuel Evain was also on the same vessel. On the night in question, he, Evain, Poirrier and Machevaux called at the Barley Mow in Southgate Street at about eleven o'clock at night. They ordered

The docks, in *Sketches of Gloucester* by A. Ward, around 1922. (Author's collection)

some beer, which was served to them, but the landlady requested them to drink up quickly and then be on their way. There were three men in the room besides themselves, one of whom was Moritz. The landlady threw part of the Frenchmen's beer under the grate. He and Machevaux rose to leave, and as they were going out of the door, the landlady pushed Machevaux against Mayon. Machevaux said to her, 'Please not to shove me so hard.'

Mayon and Machevaux left the house through the side door, then turned into the street. They waited for Evain and Poirrier, and when they appeared, Mayon heard the woman cry out, but did not know what she said.

While they were standing at the corner of the house, Moritz came out and he saw him open a knife, which he had in his belt. Mayon called out a warning, then saw Moritz stab at Evain. After Evain came out of the house, he didn't speak to Moritz, or to anyone, before he was stabbed. He only gave him one blow, and Evain put his two hands down to the lower part of his body and ran away. The prisoner and two other men then set upon Poirrier, who cried out, 'They're killing me! They're hurting me!' before falling to the ground. Mayon and Machevaux helped Poirrier get up and took him back to the *Bayonnaise*. Mayon did not see Evain again that night. Mayon was quite sure that the man in custody was the one who stabbed Evain.

Cross-examined by Mr Coren, for the defence, Mayon said they had left their vessel between seven o'clock and half past, and went first to the Berkeley Arms in Southgate Street. They had two glasses of grog each and stayed there for about half an hour. From there they went to a dance-house, the Ten Bells in Westgate Street. They had something to drink there out of a white bottle. Mayon didn't know what it was called, but the cork flew up when you took it out – it was not champagne. They stayed there for half an hour to three quarters of an hour. There was music and dancing going on,

Postcard of Southgate Street in the 1920s. (Author's collection)

but they did not dance. There were ladies there, and they talked to them. From the Ten Bells, they went to a boarding house, accompanied by some of the ladies. They were there for about half an hour, and had one glass of grog each and a quart of ale between the four of them.

At the Barley Mow, they had one quart of beer between them, supplied in a jug, with little glasses provided. Mayon did not know exactly how long they were there. He and his companions were a little excited, but not out of reason. They were not very annoyed when the landlady threw some of their drink away.

When Mr Coren asked Mayon, 'Then why did the landlady push you to get you out?' he replied, 'I cannot say.'

Joseph Machevaux corroborated his shipmate's evidence regarding the events at the Barley Mow. He said that when all four of them had come out of the house, he saw Moritz take a knife from his waist and stab at Evain, and then Evain ran away. Machevaux didn't see Poirrier being stabbed, but saw him bleeding, and afterwards he helped to take him away. He did not see Evain again that night – the following morning he had gone to the infirmary and saw his corpse. After they came out of the inn, he did not see Evain do anything to Moritz before he was stabbed. He was quite sure that Moritz was the man who stabbed Evain.

Mr Coren then cross-examined Machevaux, who said he and his companions had reached the Barley Mow at about ten minutes to eleven. They hadn't been there long when the landlady asked them to leave the house and emptied the glasses. They were not angry when she did this, and they did not say anything. After he and Mayon had gone outside, and Evain and Poirrier were at the door, he heard a noise inside the Barley Mow. It was a woman's voice, and she was crying as if she was hurt. Three strangers were in the inn at the time, as well as the two Frenchmen. Neither he nor Mayon had returned to the house. They did go back towards it, however, to pick up Poirrier. No one else was near Poirrier when they went to pick him up.

Mr Coren asked Machevaux if he had struck or pushed the landlady, or laid his hands upon her. He replied that he had not. He did not know that the landlady had been struck. When he heard the cries, Evain and Poirrier were at the door. He and Mayon had then been outside for about two minutes.

Charles Priday was the next witness. He was a boat owner who lived at Sudbrook. He was passing down Southgate Street on 3 March, a little after eleven o'clock at night. He was on the infirmary side of the street, on the opposite side to the Barley Mow. When he got near the inn, he heard raised voices inside and saw some sailors come out of the side door. Then he saw the man in custody, Moritz, come out into the alley and 'plunged one of them down with great force upon the pavement'. Priday did not see a knife. The man who was attacked rolled over several times into the gutter. He tried to get up, but could not, and two of the men went and assisted him. Priday then saw Moritz knock down another sailor and kick him, before going back into the house. Priday went to the injured man, and found that his clothes were all bloody. He stayed with the man until a policeman came. He did not see what became of the first man who was injured. When the police arrived, he went into the Barley Mow where he saw Moritz and another man, William Pidler. He did not speak to Moritz, but went back out and described him to Sergeant Tingle.

Cross-examined, Priday said he was about fifteen yards from the Barley Mow when he saw the men coming out, and that they seemed to be in

Lower Southgate Street, late 1900s. The Barley Mow was on the left-hand side, near the chapel. (Author's collection)

great confusion. A man named Price was outside the door, standing near to Moritz. When he went inside, he saw the landlady, who had a black eye. He thought it was the second or third man who came out who was first struck down, but the alley was very dark. There was about a minute between the first and the last man coming out.

The court then adjourned for half an hour, and Priday went to the infirmary. On his return, he identified the deceased as the man whom he had seen struck down and roll into the gutter.

John William Price, a boatman, was the next witness. He lived in Barley Mow Yard, Southgate Street. Price said that on the evening in question, a little after eleven, he was going from the docks to his house, and in doing so went up Southgate Street, on the same side as the Barley Mow. When he got near it, he saw five sailors, three in the street and two in the yard or alley. One of the sailors who was standing in the street was knocked down, but he didn't see who the assailant was. Moritz was outside Mrs Jones's door, in the alley. A sailor was also standing in the alley and he saw Moritz strike him, causing him to fall to the ground. He then rolled about and Moritz kicked him on the head. Moritz then returned to the Barley Mow. The side door was wide open when the incident took place, and he saw Mrs Jones and another female standing just inside. Soon afterwards, he went home. Price had also been to the infirmary and identified the dead man as being the one he saw struck first. The wounded man was the one who was kicked on the head in the alley.

Next to give evidence was Police Constable Wilkins. He deposed that he was on duty on the night of 3 March. As he was passing the dock gates at a little after eleven o'clock, a constable named Thomas Stone, who was employed by the Docks Company, called his attention to a man on the ground near the gates. He was on the footpath, leaning against the wall. Supposing him to be drunk, and hearing a disturbance at the Barley Mow, he and Stone left the man there and went up Southgate Street. Wilkins saw a man lying in the yard near the Barley Mow, and went inside and saw the accused man, Moritz. He asked him if he had either stabbed or kicked the sailor who was lying in the yard, and he said he had not. He also asked a young girl who was staying with Mrs Jones, and the servant girl, if they had seen anyone stab or kick the sailor, and they said they hadn't. Sergeant Tingle then came in.

Sergeant Tingle said that he went to the Barley Mow at about half past eleven. In the presence of Moritz, Tingle said, 'It is said outside that a man has been stabbed.' Someone answered, 'This is the man they mean,' and pointed at Moritz, who said nothing. Tingle asked him if he had a knife, and he said he hadn't. He searched him and found nothing on him.

He then went to the *Bayonnaise*, where he found one of the wounded men. He assisted in taking him to the infirmary, and afterwards returned to the Barley Mow, where he found the prisoner in bed and apprehended him. While Moritz was dressing, Tingle took hold of his hands and examined them. There was a cut on the inner part of the right hand, about an inch in length. Asked how he got it, Moritz replied, 'A Frenchman did it.' When Tingle told him that there was a man lying dead at the infirmary, and he was supposed to have stabbed and killed him, Moritz made no reply. He then took him to the police station. They had got a few paces from the inn when Moritz said, 'I will tell you all about it.' Tingle told him it was more than likely that he would be charged with murder, and he had better say nothing. He then took him to the police station and locked him up.

Dock constable Thomas Stone said that on that Monday night, he saw a man near the dock gates in Southgate Street, standing near the lamp by the weighing machine. The man then turned in towards the dock gates. Stone followed him in order to let him into the docks. The man stood on the footpath for a moment or two, and then fell backwards. Stone picked him up and sat him against the railings. He did not speak, and Stone had the impression that he was drunk. He then went with PC Wilkins to the Barley Mow, before returning to where he had left the man. He found him lying on the ground, face downwards. With assistance, he took him to the infirmary, where he helped the house surgeon undress him. They found his clothes were saturated with blood, and his socks and boots sodden.

Deputy Chief Constable Griffin was then called, and said he had gone to the infirmary the day before and saw the body, and took possession of the dead man's clothes, which he now produced. They were saturated with blood, and there was a cut on his trousers and undergarments on the right-hand side of the groin area. The blood had run down his legs into his boots.

Mr Cole, the house surgeon at the infirmary, said Evain had been brought in at about twenty past twelve on Monday night. He was bleeding from a wound in the front of the upper part of the right thigh. The wound was about two inches long and three to four inches deep. Evain was insensible when he was brought in, and had lost a lot of blood. He died about twenty minutes after his admission.

The evidence of the prosecution being concluded, Otto Moritz was formally charged with murder and committed to take his trial at the next assizes. The sitting had lasted for over five hours.

The next day, Thursday, 6 March, Otto Moritz was brought before the magistrates again, this time for the attack on Emile Poirrier. The injured man was too ill to leave the infirmary, so the magistrates went there to take his evidence. Through an interpreter, he told the same story as his companions of how they went to the Barley Mow and were asked to leave quickly. When asked by Mr Taynton who had left the inn first, Poirrier could not remember. He thought he had come out second from last. After he came out, he was struck down, and then Moritz stabbed him in the back of the

The infirmary in Southgate Street. (Author's collection)

head. He was kicked and knocked about as he lay on the ground, and lost his senses. He didn't know how he received his second wound.

He had not said anything to Moritz before he left the inn, and had not quarrelled with him. He saw the landlady throw their beer away, but didn't hear any angry words spoken. As well as the Frenchmen and Moritz, there was another man, the landlady and her sister in the house. He didn't see the landlady get struck in the eye. He and his companions had all had a little drop to drink, but they were not 'deranged'. He was quite sure that Moritz was the man who attacked him.

Mr Cole said Poirrier had been brought to the infirmary between twelve and one o'clock. He had a wound on the back of his head, about two inches long and down to the bone, and a smaller wound in the muscles of his back, on the left side of the spine. He was also bruised on various parts of his body. The wounds in the head and back were clean cut and could not have been caused by anything other than a sharp-pointed instrument. He said that the wound in the head was not of a dangerous character.

The magistrates then went to the police station to hear the remainder of the evidence. Etienne Mayon was the first witness. He repeated the evidence he had given on the previous day as to going to the Barley Mow and seeing the prisoner attack Evain. He then saw Moritz strike Poirrier, but could not see whether it was a punch or a stab. He saw Moritz strike Poirrier while he was on the ground, but couldn't see what he struck him with. Moritz then went back into the Barley Mow, and the doors were shut. Mayon and Machevaux helped Poirrier up and took him to their vessel. Afterwards they assisted in taking him to the infirmary. Joseph Machevaux corroborated this evidence, adding that back on board the *Bayonnaise*, they found that Poirrier was covered with blood.

Charles Priday repeated his former evidence, and said he saw Moritz knock down one man outside the front door, then go into the alley and knock down a second man. He saw nothing in the prisoner's hand. John Price said he saw the prisoner knock Poirrier down and stamp on his head with his left foot. He also saw a knife in the prisoner's left hand.

Deputy Chief Constable Griffin said he went to the infirmary on Wednesday and collected some clothes belonging to Poirrier. These were very bloody – especially the two shirts – about the neck and back.

Moritz was committed to stand trial for wounding Poirrier.

On the same Thursday, an inquest was held on the body of Emanuel Evain in the Board Room at the infirmary. Thomas Stone was the first witness. He deposed to finding Evain near the entrance gates to the docks, opposite the Albion Hotel, and assisting in taking him to the infirmary.

Etienne Mayon, in describing the attack on Evain, said he thought the prisoner had a knife in his right hand, and he saw him strike him in the lower part of the body. Evain put his hands down to where he had received the blow, then ran away. Joseph Machevaux repeated the evidence he had previously given to the magistrates.

John Price and Charles Priday also repeated their evidence. Price added that he saw a knife in the prisoner's hand, which had been up his sleeve. The knife was four or five inches long. He admitted that he had not previously mentioned the length of the knife, or that Moritz had it up his sleeve.

Next to be called was a new witness, William Pidler, master of a vessel and a resident of Bideford. He said that on Monday night he had gone to the Barley Mow at about ten to eleven. He saw some foreign sailors in the kitchen, and all was quiet. He went into the bar and called for a glass of ale. He saw a crowd of sailors going out of the door of the kitchen after Mrs Jones told them to leave. He heard one of them call out in French that he was being pushed. He afterwards heard a woman scream out, and then within a minute the house appeared to have been cleared of all the sailors. Then the police arrived.

Mrs Ann Jones was the next to give evidence. She said she was a widow and kept the Barley Mow inn in Southgate Street, and that she also took in lodgers. Moritz had slept at the house for seven or eight nights before the evening in question. On that night, he had been in the kitchen nearly all evening with several others, who she thought were all Germans.

The Frenchmen came in at about ten to eleven. They ordered a pot of beer, which was fetched by the servant. They sat down in the kitchen at a table, away from the others. Captain Pidler was in the bar and reminded her that it was eleven o'clock. By her clock, it was five minutes to eleven, but to be sure she sent her sister to the Albion Hotel, to ascertain the exact time. She then ran into the kitchen to clear out the people. She thought there were four or five Germans on one side, and the four Frenchmen on the other.

She went to the Frenchmen first, because they had begun to sing and appeared rather quarrelsome. Also, in the past she had experienced difficulty in getting French sailors to leave. She asked them to drink up quickly, because the policeman would be there soon. She made them understand by 'motions'. They said, 'Oh, plenty time,' in English, and began to sing. They did not drink up, and she said she would not get into trouble for them, and threw two portions of their beer away. She wasn't sure if the Germans had gone then, but she believed they left while she was throwing the beer away. Then there was only Moritz, herself, her servant and another woman left in the kitchen. Captain Pidler was in the bar.

She shut the front door because it was eleven o'clock, and opened the side door to let out the Frenchmen. She didn't know who went out first, but they left one at a time. The last one was a short man, with a light moustache. He stood at the door as if he wanted to say something, so she pushed him a little bit. As she did so, another man ran up to her and struck her with his fist in her eye. She fell down insensible, and was taken upstairs. She did not see Moritz leave the kitchen, because she was upstairs for twenty minutes.

Asked if Moritz was in the habit of wearing a knife in his belt, she replied that he may have done so, but she had never seen him with one. She did not know anything about a knife being used that night. She did not know what happened in the yard; 'I could not see, because my eye was so bad.' When she came back downstairs, Moritz was sitting on a chair in the kitchen. She thought it was the tallest of the Frenchmen who had struck her.

Machevaux was then called in, and she identified him as the one who had hit her. Deputy Chief Constable Griffin said that Mrs Jones had previously claimed that it was the dead man who struck her. She said she had thought that at first, but now she was positive that Machevaux was the man. Mayon was called in, and she said he was the last man who left the house and the one she had pushed.

Mrs Jones's sister and the servant girl were called, but their evidence was not considered significant and they were not sworn in to give evidence. Caroline Smith, an elderly woman who lived in Royal Oak Yard, was the next witness. She had been in the Barley Mow that Monday night, at about eleven o'clock. Contradicting the landlady's evidence, she said that Moritz and the servant girl were the only ones in the kitchen besides herself. Some

French sailors came in and had some beer. She heard the landlady ask them to leave. This they did after some trouble. As the last left she heard Mrs Jones scream, and her sister came into the kitchen, saying Mrs Jones had a black eye. Smith went into the bar, and Mrs Jones said one of the French sailors had done it. She remained with her in the bar for a few minutes, then they all went into the kitchen, where Moritz was standing. Smith remained there a minute or two, then went and looked out of the side door. She saw some men standing there and one lying on the ground. She shut the door and returned to the kitchen, where Mrs Jones remained, until there was a knock on the door and the police arrived.

Asked whether Mrs Jones had been anywhere besides the bar and the kitchen, Smith said she could not swear, but if the landlady had gone any-where else, she must have done so very quickly. She did not know whether Moritz had gone outside, but he might have done while she was in the bar with the landlady. She had never seen Moritz with a knife. There had been no confusion in the bar; everything had been pretty quiet. Mrs Jones was conscious after she received the blow.

Jane Price, the sister of Mrs Jones, then gave her evidence to the inquest. She said she was in the bar when the four sailors left. After they were gone she heard her sister cry out, and she went to her. Finding her on the ground, she and the servant helped her up and took her upstairs. Price came down and went into the bar, and Moritz was then in the kitchen. She stayed in the bar for a short time and then went into the kitchen.

Deputy Chief Constable Griffin then produced the deceased man's clothes, and Mr Cole repeated his evidence as to the injury Evain had received. He added that he had now carried out a post-mortem examination and found that the wound had been caused by some sharp, pointed instrument, which had pierced the femoral vein and was the cause of death. He added that all the other organs were healthy, and if medical assistance had been rendered immediately after the wound was caused, the man's life would in all probability have been saved.

The Coroner summed up the case for the jury, who then conferred for a few minutes, before returning a verdict of wilful murder against Moritz. Through the foreman, they also expressed their opinion that it would be desirable, if possible, to prevent sailors coming onshore with their knives,

Gloucester from above, with the docks in the foreground. (Author's collection)

adding that they believed notices to that effect were issued in Gloucester several years ago.

On 1 April 1873, the assizes opened in Gloucester, and the trial of Otto Moritz began on Monday, 7 April, before Judge Sir George Honyman. The case for the prosecution was presented by Mr Matthews, QC, while the prisoner was defended by Mr Powell, QC. The trial opened with the presentation of the case for the prosecution, and the surviving French sailors and the witnesses were examined. Because of delays in interpreting the evidence, the prosecution had not finished presenting their case by half past six in the evening, so the members of the jury were locked up for the night, and the trial resumed the next day.

On the second day of the trial, the four principal witnesses were Mrs Jones, the landlady, Mrs Price, her sister, a servant, and Caroline Smith. All of them were examined at the request of the judge. Each of them insisted that Moritz could not have been the one who inflicted the fatal wound on Evain, because he hadn't left the kitchen at the time of the quarrel. However, when they were cross-examined, Smith, Jones and Price all contradicted each other's evidence.

Mr Matthews then summed up the case for the prosecution, arguing that it had been conclusively shown that it was the prisoner's hand which had inflicted the fatal blow, that there was no sufficient justification for his conduct, and that the jury must therefore fearlessly discharge their duty and find the prisoner guilty of the graver charge – in other words, find Moritz guilty of murder.

Mr Powell then made an earnest speech in defence of the prisoner, pointing out that no one had actually seen Moritz stab Evain. He hadn't quarrelled with the sailors, and so had no reason to attack them in such a bloodthirsty manner; it was just as probable that one of the other men who were in the Barley Mow at the time had done it. If Moritz really had inflicted the fatal blow, then it was obviously in self-defence, because when he came to the aid of the landlady, there were four of them against one of him. Therefore this was justifiable homicide, and Moritz should be acquitted.

The jury absented themselves for forty-five minutes, and on their return announced that they found Otto Moritz guilty of manslaughter. The judge then sentenced him to ten years' penal servitude. The prison registers recorded that on 28 April 1873, Moritz was sent to Pentonville Prison in London, where he was to serve his sentence.

CASE TWO 1875

'HE DID SOCIETY NO GOOD'

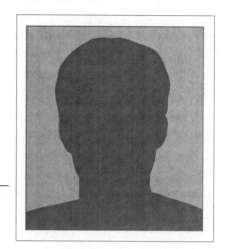

Suspect:	George Clements
Age:	Thirty-two
Charge:	Attempted Murder

In May 1873, a by-election in Gloucester was declared following the resignation of William Price, one of the city's two Liberal Members of Parliament. The Liberal Party put up Thomas Robinson, a Gloucester corn merchant, as their candidate, while the Conservatives put forward another corn merchant, William Killigrew Wait. The latter was based in Bristol and lived in Clifton, but was an employer in Gloucester, having a warehouse at the docks. The Liberals were hopeful of a victory for their candidate, but the Tories had an energetic supporter in Mr Edward Tew-Smith, a Gloucester town councillor, and an active agent in Mr Taynton, from a Gloucester firm of solicitors.

Both parties campaigned vigorously in the time leading up to polling day, with the nominated candidates addressing numerous public meetings, and their respective agents sending canvassers out to knock on doors in all the streets of the city and its suburbs. Intense excitement prevailed, made more so by the fact that this election was to be only the second one in Gloucester to use the recently introduced system of secret balloting.

The election was held on Thursday, 8 May, and both sides exerted a great deal of effort in getting voters to the various polling stations. The atmosphere in the city centre was lively, but the proceedings were conducted in good temper. The Conservatives had their headquarters at the Bell Hotel in Southgate Street, and in the evening, while the votes were being counted, about eighty gentlemen sat down to a meal there, presided over by Mr Taynton. The result of the election was announced from the steps of Shire Hall at a quarter to nine. The winner was the Tory candidate – William Killigrew Wait – by a majority of eighty-five votes. Wait gave his victory speech from a window at the Bell Hotel.

Gloucester had been investigated on previous occasions for engaging in corrupt practices during elections, and on 3 June, the supporters of Thomas Robinson presented a petition against the election of Wait. This meant that before he could officially take his seat in parliament, an electoral commission had to hold an inquiry to investigate the complaints made against him and his team.

The specific charges made by the Liberals against their opponents were of bribery, treating, undue influence and personation. Fourteen people working for Wait through his agent, Taynton, were charged with bribing fourteen others. In addition, fourteen people (who were not all the same ones as on the previous charge) were alleged to have 'treated' fifty-three voters at fifteen different public houses between 1 and 9 May 1873. Thirty-six people were said to have been unduly influenced by seven others, besides many not named who received a card headed 'Gloucester Election, Thursday, May 8, 1873', and containing the words, 'any other mark upon the ballot

Shire Hall, in *Six Engravings of Public Buildings in the City of Gloucester* by A.N. Smith. (Gloucestershire Archives, D9795/2/4/5)

paper than a cross against the name of Wait will invalidate your vote.'
There were also three charges of personation (a person pretending to be
someone else in order to vote), and eight of Wait's agents were charged
with aiding and abetting in these personations.

The inquiry was held between 15 and 18 July 1873 at the Crown Court,
Shire Hall, before Mr Justice Blackburn. Many witnesses were called to give
evidence during the course of the inquiry, and among them was one man
who attracted the particular interest of the local press. George Clements was
brought into the courtroom from the nearby prison, where he was in custody
awaiting trial on a charge of receiving stolen goods. He was a chimney sweep
by trade, and had a long criminal record. A man with a violent temper, he had
been in Gloucester Prison on many occasions before now, and was a familiar
figure in the courts. On this occasion, though, Clements was not charged with
any offence, but was merely questioned concerning his part in helping to
canvass for the Tory candidate during the recent election.

Clements said that in the days leading up to the election he was 'at large'
and working on his own account for his party, 'the Blues'. He knew
Mr Tew-Smith, the Tory agent, and went about with him, canvassing in
the Colombia Street district, which was near his home in Union Street.
He was with Mr Tew-Smith on election day, and said he was chosen to go
along with him. The judge then declared that he had not been chosen by
anybody, but he chose himself – a remark which caused laughter in the
court. Clements said he had also canvassed with Mr Taylor, who was his
landlord, and Mr Anderson, who ran the Suffolk Arms. After the election,
he had been given twenty-five shillings for taking circulars out. That was
all the money he received, although he thought he should have got more
(laughter). He didn't suppose he would get it now (more laughter).

Clements was questioned more specifically on the allegation of treating.
The petitioners had complained that during the election, a large number
of public houses had opened up which supported the Tory cause. In these
establishments, liquor was distributed freely as an encouragement to voters
to put their cross against the name of Mr Wait. One of these public houses
was the Suffolk Arms, and the petitioners said the Tories held committee
meetings in an upstairs room there, at which Tew-Smith and John Butt,
another Tory agent, were active.

Clements said that he knew the Suffolk Arms, but was never in an upstairs room there during election time. He had seen Mr Butt and others there, but couldn't say it was a committee, or whether they talked about election matters. He had seen people drinking there at election time, but he didn't know who paid. He had seen some of the men whose names were mentioned as having been treated in return for their votes drinking in the Suffolk Arms, but he couldn't see if they paid for their drinks or not. He had seen 'quarts and quarts' of beer on the table, and had seen cans of beer brought in. He did not see any person pay for this beer. He drank some milk and rum there on the morning of the election, in the presence of Mr Tew-Smith, but Clements did not pay for it. He heard someone say, 'Put it down, it's all right,' but he believed Mr Tew-Smith was in another room at the time.

Clements continued that he had had no conversation with Thomas Anderson, the landlord of the Suffolk Arms, about the drink that was had at election time; at least he couldn't remember it. Anderson had told him he would give him 'a drop of something', but what was the cause of saying so, he could not tell. Clements was asked if he knew Anderson had a bill that wasn't paid, and he replied that he did not know Anderson's business.

Having finished giving his evidence, Clements was taken back to his prison cell, and the questioning of other witnesses continued. Thomas Anderson was called and was asked if he had told George Clements that his bill for the drinks given to Tory voters was over £28, and when he was paid, he would give Clements a dinner and a bottle of wine. Anderson said he did remember giving Clements a dinner, but he liked wine too much himself to give away a bottle. He denied that he had made up a bill for beer and spirits supplied during the election, or that anyone had paid him anything.

On the next day, having considered all the evidence, the commission declared that the petitioners had lost their case, and William Killigrew Wait was declared to be duly elected.

Two weeks after the election inquiry, Gloucester held its Quarter Sessions, and the case for which George Clements had been awaiting trial was heard. Alice Jones, who was a prostitute, was charged with stealing a watch and chain and £2 from a man named Hiam, while George Clements and Harriet Gregory were charged with receiving the stolen property. At the time of the incident, Clements and Gregory were living as man and wife at 25 Union Street. Alice took Hiam to the house, where he stayed the night, and the next morning he found that his watch and money were missing. He reported the theft to the police and all three miscreants were arrested. Jones admitted stealing Hiam's property, and Clements and Gregory said they had disposed of the watch, which Gregory had sold to a Dutch sailor. Jones was sentenced to four months for the theft and Gregory to three months for receiving, but Clements, who had several previous offences, was sentenced to twelve months' imprisonment and two years under police supervision upon his release.

George Clements was born in Gloucester in 1844, the son of George and Harriet Clements. His father was a chimney sweep and the family lived in the Quay Street area of the city. George Clements junior was the youngest of four children, having one sister, Mary, and two brothers, Joseph and Samuel. His first recorded brush with the law had come at the age of fifteen, when in December 1859 he was imprisoned for a couple of days for an unnamed felony. No doubt the magistrate who committed him thought that this would teach the boy a lesson, but unfortunately it had no good effect on the young Clements: in 1862 he was sentenced to two months' hard labour for assaulting his own mother.

George Clements senior died in 1864, and it is possible that after she was widowed, Mrs Clements had made ends meet by taking in lodgers, some of them of a dubious character. In July 1866, George was once more up before the magistrates at the city petty sessions, charged with assaulting Emily Parry, who was lodging with his mother in nearby Quay Lane. A man calling himself a 'gentleman farmer' had gone to the house of Mrs Clements with Parry, where he paid for six shillings-worth of brandy. Clements said that Parry had put her crinoline over the farmer's head and picked his pockets, and that he (Clements), was trying to stop her. Parry said that it was Clements who wanted to rob the farmer, and she tried to stop him, a result of which he had struck her and kicked her. Clements was fined twenty shillings, plus costs.

In November 1870, George Clements found himself in serious trouble when he was charged with the manslaughter of a woman named Sarah

Ann Price. Price was a young woman from Monmouthshire, who had come to Gloucester with her illegitimate daughter, aged about seven years old. She had taken lodgings at 25 Union Street, where Clements was then living with his wife, Sarah. Union Street at that time was described in the local newspaper as 'one of the lowest parts of the city'.

On the night of 28 October 1870, Mrs Clements, Price and another female lodger had waited up for George, and when he came home very late and found no supper prepared for him, he quarrelled with his wife, who was sitting on a sofa with Sarah Ann Price beside her. Clements picked up an ornamental shell with jagged edges and threw it at his wife, who dodged out of the way. The shell hit Price on the forehead and blood flowed from the resulting wound. Immediately contrite, Clements paid a chemist for medicine and bandages, but Price and her daughter left the house a couple of days later. She seemed none the worse for her injury at first, but about a week later she was found slumped in a doorway by the police. She was sent to a tramps' lodging house and was attended by the Union surgeon, but she died of an abscess on the brain. George Clements was found guilty of manslaughter at the Gloucester Assizes in April 1871 and was sentenced to eight months' imprisonment.

Gloucester Prison's gatehouse, through which George Clements passed many times. (Jill Evans)

After serving this sentence, Clements was not out of the courts for long, as in 1872 he was jailed for one month for assaulting a police officer. Later in the same year, there was evidence that he was venturing out of Gloucester to commit crimes, because he made an appearance in September at Berkeley Police Court, along with his wife, Sarah, and two girls, Lilly Cooke and Catherine Pritchard. They were charged with stealing £6 in gold from Henry Richard Bailey, a navvy, at the Sharpness Hotel. Bailey was reluctant to give evidence and failed to prove his case, so all four were discharged.

In March 1873, Clements was back before the magistrates at Gloucester, on a charge of assaulting his wife. By this time, Clements was being described in the local press as 'an old offender' who was 'well-known at the court'. Sarah had refused to press charges, but from her statement and that of a police constable, it appeared that Clements had returned home in a drunken state, knocked his wife down and attempted to throttle

'knocked his wife down and attempted to throttle her'

her. Knowing that his violence was associated with his alcohol consumption, Clements now assured the magistrates that he would sign the pledge (to stay teetotal) if they would let him go. On this promise, and on finding sureties to keep the peace for three months, he was discharged.

On 29 July 1873, Clements was tried at the Quarter Sessions on the charge of receiving stolen goods, and was imprisoned for twelve months. He was released from prison in July 1874. The two-year supervision order imposed upon him didn't stop him from getting into trouble again, as in January 1875 he was fined for being drunk and disorderly, and in March of that same year he was jailed for six months for assaulting his wife and a police officer.

On his release from prison in September 1875, Clements managed to get himself a job as a corn porter at the docks, and announced his intention to reform. However, he was soon drinking again and by November he was, once again, in serious trouble.

On 29 November 1875, Clements sub-let his house at 25 Union Street to two prostitutes, Sarah (known as Sally) Bryant and Lilly Cooke. Clements already knew Cooke, who was one of the women he appeared with at Berkeley Police Court in 1872. The women were to pay rent of five shillings a week, on the understanding that Clements could sleep at the house when he wanted. Clements apparently told Cooke that he was willing to let her off paying her share of the rent, and on the night of 29 November he spent the night in her room.

On 1 December, Cooke and Bryant went to the Vaults Bar at the Fleece Inn in Westgate Street, and Cooke had a drink there with a young man named Lapworth. Clements came into the bar and saw Lapworth buy Cooke some potatoes. Jealousy flaring up inside him, he told her that if Lapworth slept with her that night, there would be murder in the house. On the following night, keen to make things up after their quarrel, Clements knocked on Cooke's bedroom door, but she refused to let him in.

On the evening of Friday, 3 December, Clements accompanied the two women to the Fleece Inn. They were joined there by William Davis, who was a fishmonger, and by a German sailor. Clements, perhaps in an attempt to make Cooke jealous, treated Bryant to some grog and gave her sixpence. Bryant, loyal to her friend, gave Cooke the sixpence in front of Clements.

An old postcard of The Vaults bar under the Fleece Inn, at one time known as The Monk's Retreat. (Author's collection)

Westgate Street in the 1900s. The Fleece Hotel is the sixth building on the left.
(Author's collection)

He then treated a girl known as 'Brummie Emma' to a drink. This did
provoke Cooke and she had a fight with her rival. Lapworth came into the
bar and Clements quarrelled with him, then swore at Cooke, kicked her,
and struck her in the face. Cooke said to her friend, 'Oh, Sally, I am afraid
to go home, there'll be murder in the house, you watch it.' Later, Clements
calmed down and put his hand round her waist and gave her half a crown.

Cooke and Clements left the Fleece before Bryant, and went home. Just
after she had got to her bedroom, Clements came to the door. She told him
that she would not sleep with him because he was married, and started
to put on her outdoor things, deciding it would be best to leave the house.
Clements said, 'I'll be hanged for a better woman than my wife, that's you,
and I'll murder you tonight.' Cooke cried, 'Oh George, what for?' and
Clements replied, 'Because I love you, you cow!'

He then grabbed hold of her and pulled a knife from his pocket, which
he held across her throat. She put her hand up and felt it cut her finger.
Frightened for her life, she turned quickly, and Clements thrust the blade
under her left shoulder, and then she heard the blade snap. She felt blood
pouring from the wound and cried out, 'Oh George, you have stabbed me!'

Clements said nothing, but pulled the broken knife out of her and left the room. However, he soon came back and, kneeling by the bed and tearing at his hair, asked for God's forgiveness. He begged Cooke not to tell anyone what he had done, and offered to give her furniture and money if she didn't report him.

At this point, Sarah Bryant returned to the house with William Davis. The two went upstairs and found Cooke and Clements in the bedroom. Clements offered to send for a doctor and produced seven shillings to pay for one. He and Davis took some pictures off the wall, undusted for years, and used some cobwebs from behind them to try to stay the bleeding. This didn't work, and Lilly Cooke had to be taken to the infirmary. The police were called in, and George Clements was arrested.

On the following Monday, Clements was brought before the Gloucester magistrates. Cooke, whose real name was Mary Elizabeth Solmon, was too ill to attend, being still in the infirmary, but the evidence of William Davis and of Sarah Bryant was taken. They said that when they got home on Friday night, they found that Cooke had been stabbed in the back and was bleeding freely. They all tried to stop the bleeding and when it was proposed to send for a surgeon, Clements produced seven shillings for the fee. The surgeon didn't come and Clements left, saying he would go to his aunt's in Newent. Cooke asked him to kiss her, and they kissed each other

The infirmary, in *Six Engravings of Public Buildings in the City of Gloucester* by A.N. Smith. (Gloucestershire Archives, D9795/2/4/5)

several times, and he got down on his knees by the bedside and prayed that he might be forgiven.

Clements was remanded for a week. He claimed that what Bryant and Davis had said was untrue, and when they came back after the adjournment, he would have someone to speak for him.

A week later, the inquiry continued and the proceedings started at the infirmary, where Lilly Cooke, who was still too ill to attend at Shire Hall, gave her evidence. George Clements was present and he asked her whether she hadn't promised him that she would keep from other men if he let her have the house, but she denied this. The inquiry then continued at Shire Hall, where the policeman who arrested Clements told of how he had found a bloody knife under a chest of drawers in the house. No one appeared to speak for Clements and he was charged with stabbing Cooke, with intent to murder her, and was remanded in custody, to take his trial at the next assizes.

Once again, George Clements was taken through the gatehouse of Gloucester Prison, as he had been so many times already in his thirty-two years. He would have been very familiar with the routine as a new prisoner entering the gaol, where he was washed and examined by a doctor, and his description carefully recorded in the prison register. He was described as being five feet four and a half inches tall, with dark brown hair, blue eyes, a long face and a fresh complexion. He had scars on the left side of his forehead, on both eyebrows, and on his left cheek. There was another scar on the back of his leg, and he also had burn scars on the left side of his stomach and the back of his left arm.

In April 1876, the assizes began at Gloucester, presided over by Mr Justice Montagu Smith. The trial of George Clements took place on 15 April. Mr Griffiths prosecuted, while Clements was defended by Mr Sawyer.

Mr Griffiths opened the case and his first witness was Lilly Cooke. She recounted the tale of what happened on that Friday night in December, and told the court that she had been in the infirmary for four weeks after the stabbing, and had not yet fully recovered from the wound. The clothes she was wearing on that night and the knife used to stab her were produced.

Sarah Bryant and William Davis then gave their evidence. They were followed by Mr Sampson, the house surgeon at the infirmary, who said Lilly Cooke had a clean-cut wound, about three-quarters of an inch in length and just over an inch in depth. The wound was midway between the centre of the back and the right shoulder blade, and penetrated near the serous membrane of the right lung. It was a dangerous wound and must have been caused by great violence.

Mr Sawyer, for the defence, did not wish to cross-examine the witnesses. He said he did not deny that the prisoner, Clements, had inflicted the wound, and the only question for the jury was what offence he should be found guilty of. He disputed the idea that Clements had intended to murder the girl, because if he had wished to do so, he had ample opportunity. His conduct afterwards showed that he had no such intention. Because of this, Mr Sawyer submitted that the jury would be justified in finding the prisoner guilty of unlawful wounding.

The judge directed the jury to consider whether there was anything in the case which would warrant them in returning a verdict for a lesser offence than that of unlawfully wounding. In reference to the words used by the prisoner before the wound

Sketch of Pentonville Prison's gateway, from *The Criminal Prisons of London* by Mayhew and Binney, 1862. (Author's collection)

Sketch of a cell in Pentonville Prison, from *The Criminal Prisons of London* by Mayhew and Binney, 1862. (Author's collection)

was inflicted, he argued that when a man was in drink he might use certain expressions which the jury could consider to be less significant than they would otherwise have been. In this case, there was no evidence that the prisoner was drunk, although he had been drinking.

In considering whether the wound was inflicted with intent to murder or to inflict grievous bodily harm, they must look at the weapon used, at the part of the body which was attacked and at the consequences of the act. The jury retired before returning a verdict of guilty of wounding with intent to murder.

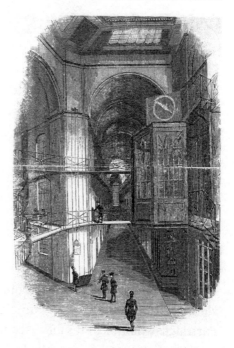

Sketch of Pentonville Prison in the *Illustrated London News*, 7 January 1843. (Author's collection)

In passing sentence, the judge said he thoroughly concurred with the verdict. Addressing Clements, he said he had before him a very sad record of his life. He then read out the long list of his previous convictions. It was clear that imprisonment did him no good, that he did society no good, and under the circumstances it was his duty to pass upon him a very severe sentence. Clements was lucky that the woman who was the subject of his attack had survived, otherwise he would have been facing a death sentence. As it was, he sentenced Clements to twenty years' penal servitude.

George Clements was taken back to Gloucester Prison, but soon afterwards he was removed to Pentonville Prison. At that notoriously harsh prison, he would spend the first nine months of his sentence in solitary confinement (as all prisoners at Pentonville were), only leaving his cell for exercise and to attend the prison chapel.

SOLVED

CASE THREE 1882

'THAT UNHAPPY LUNATIC'

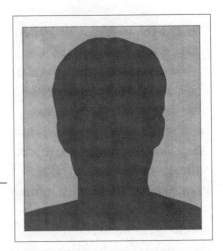

Suspect: William Hawkins
Age: Thirty-eight
Charge: Manslaughter

On 13 April 1882, the name of Walter Partridge was entered in the admissions register of the County Lunatic Asylum in Horton Road, Wotton. Partridge, who was in his fifties, came from the village of Sheepscombe, near Stroud. He was a carpenter by trade, who had also been the clerk of the parish church for a number of years, and not long before he entered the asylum, he had been running the village post office with his wife. About two months after he was admitted, on Monday, 12 June 1882, Partridge died. He had not been in good physical health and it was assumed that he had died of natural causes. However, when Dr Thomas, the asylum's assistant medical officer briefly examined the body before it was sent to the mortuary, he noticed that several of Partridge's ribs appeared to be broken.

On 14 June, an inquest was opened into the sudden death of Walter Partridge. Mr Toller, the medical superintendent of the asylum, was the first to give evidence. He said Partridge had been diagnosed as suffering from 'general paralysis of the insane' – a term which in the nineteenth century was applied to many patients suffering from dementia, seizures, delusions and other symptoms. He was, said Toller, exceedingly restless and a very troublesome patient.

A post-mortem examination had been carried out on Tuesday morning, in Toller's presence. On opening up the chest, it was found that the heart was much enlarged with valvular disease. Seven of the ribs on the right

Sheepscombe, home of Walter Partridge. (Author's collection)

side of the body were fractured. Examination of the head revealed extensive effusion on the brain, and that the brain tissue was rather soft.

Toller concluded that the serious effusion of the brain, along with the diseased heart, were the primary causes of death, but the fractures of the ribs had no doubt accelerated death. The patient would probably not have lived for more than a few days more, if his ribs had not been fractured. Toller believed that the injury to the ribs could have been inflicted up to ten hours before death. He told the Coroner that he had taken great pains to obtain information from warders and patients, but they revealed nothing which might explain how the injuries to Partridge were caused.

Dr Thomas said he was sent to attend Partridge a little before ten o'clock on Monday morning. He found Partridge in the day room, where he was sitting down with his head bent on his chest. He was conscious, but breathing very slowly and the doctor was unable to find a pulse. Partridge died about five minutes later. Thomas saw nothing at the time which made him suspect that any violence had been used.

About twenty minutes later, when the body had been washed and laid out, Thomas had noticed that Partridge had suffered some sort of injury to his ribs. He cautioned the attendants to be very careful when moving the body, as he was anxious to keep it in the same condition as when death occurred. He asked the attendant in charge, Stephens, if any violence had taken place, to which he replied, 'None that I know of'.

Dr Thomas agreed with Toller's evidence as to the results of the post-mortem and the cause of death, but he believed the broken ribs must have been received within a few hours before Partridge died. He could hardly understand how a person with these injuries could have gone about without showing symptoms of pain, although persons in Partridge's condition were not so sensitive in their expression of pain as sane people.

He had seen the deceased on Sunday night, at about half past eight. His attention had been called to Partridge by the attendant Hopkins, who said this patient had been very restless and excitable all day, and had been breaking glass. Thomas asked him how he was and Partridge replied that he had never felt better in his life, and was in no pain whatsoever.

Asked about Partridge's behaviour in the asylum, Dr Thomas replied that he had been very mischievous and dirty, and would often steal other patients' food. He had heard them abuse him for doing so, but he had never seen another patient strike him.

Frederick Charles Stephens stated that he was in charge of Ward 5, where Partridge was placed, during the day. Ward 5 had twelve single rooms, a padded room, a bathroom and three dormitories. The twelve single rooms opened onto a corridor. Partridge used to sleep in a single room by himself.

On the morning of Monday, 12 June, he went into Partridge's room to wake him up, but found him standing by the wall. They said good morning to each other and Stephens told Partridge to get dressed and handed him his clothes, but then realised that he was 'in a very dirty state'. He therefore told attendant William Hawkins to bathe him and watch him dress. He was in the dormitory, eighteen or twenty yards away from the bathroom, while Hawkins and Partridge were in there. He saw Partridge just outside the bathroom door at about seven o'clock, when he was getting dressed, supervised by Hawkins. Stephens saw him again about fifteen minutes later, dressed and walking beside Hawkins to the day room. He next saw him at a quarter to eight, sitting at the breakfast table in the day room, and he seemed all right then.

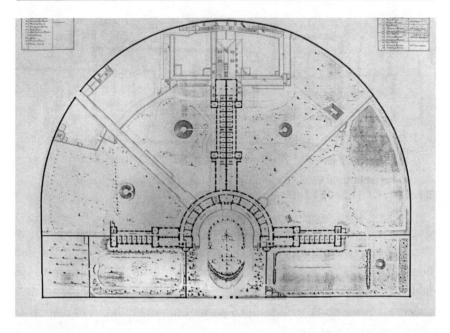

Ground-floor plan of Gloucester Lunatic Asylum, by T. Fulljames, around 1842. (Gloucestershire Archives, D12733/1)

At about ten minutes to ten, Hawkins came and asked him if he thought Partridge was fit to go out to the airing court. Stephens asked what was wrong with him, and Hawkins took him to the day room. He found Partridge sitting on a locker and leaning against the wall. He said, 'Why, Hawkins, this man's a-dying!' and told him to fetch Tom Dent, the head attendant. Hawkins was gone longer than expected, so Stephens sent attendant Hopkins for Dr Thomas. The doctor ordered Partridge to be taken to the dormitory, where he died shortly after. Later, when it became known about Partridge's injuries, Hawkins said perhaps the body was dropped when it was taken to the mortuary.

Stephens had also seen Partridge on the previous day, and was with him more or less from six in the morning until two o'clock in the afternoon. He showed no sign of being in pain. Stephens said he had never heard that Partridge had been subjected to violence by other patients and knew nothing that could account for the broken ribs.

Thomas Dancey, master tailor at the asylum, was also an attendant for half a day on alternate Sundays. On Sunday, 11 June, he was on duty

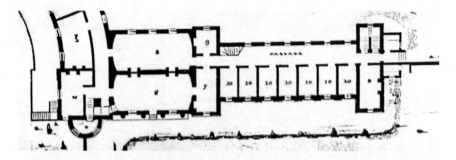

Close-up of a corridor, from the ground-floor plan of Gloucester Lunatic Asylum,
T. Fulljames, around 1842. (Gloucestershire Archives, D12733/1)

from nine in the morning until half past twelve. Partridge was walking in the yard with the other patients and seemed fine then, but earlier he had been breaking the glass of the pump-room windows. At half past twelve, he left Partridge in the care of attendant Knight. There was some disagreement between Partridge and a patient named Wilkins, and another attendant separated them.

William Hawkins said he saw Partridge at about six o'clock on Monday morning. He was in a dirty condition and Hawkins took him to the bathroom. He got into the bath without help and Hawkins didn't see any marks of violence on him. He watched Partridge get dressed then walked with him to the day room. Hawkins hadn't heard of anything which might account for Partridge's injuries, but on the previous day, at about five o'clock in the evening, as he was leaving the day room, he heard Partridge fall. He went back in and picked him up, sitting him on a seat by the table. Partridge couldn't have had a quarrel with another patient because Hawkins would have heard. He saw him safely to bed at about nine o'clock on Sunday night, then next saw him on Monday morning.

Three other attendants, Jennings, Cam and Dyke, also gave evidence. They could throw no light on how Partridge came by his injuries. The Coroner then called in several patients, two of whom said they were always treated kindly by the attendants. The others made statements which were vague and unreliable. The Coroner remarked on the fact that the deceased man had received very serious injuries, yet no one seemed to know how he came by them. The hearing had now been going on for six hours and the inquest was adjourned to allow more time for further inquiries to be made.

On Wednesday, 21 June, the inquest resumed. The jury visited the asylum and viewed the bathroom, day room and the bedroom used by Partridge, and also visited the pump-house, where the deceased had broken some windows on the day before his death.

Dr Thomas was recalled and was questioned more about Partridge's injuries. He believed there must have been direct pressure on the chest to have caused the fractures. Asked whether an attendant might have applied a knee to the chest to restrain the patient, Dr Thomas said this practice was not permitted at the asylum.

Dr William Kebbell, senior assistant medical officer at the asylum, thought Partridge's injuries might have been sustained within six hours

'considerable force on the chest'

of death, but probably less. He believed the injuries were caused by considerable force on the chest, applied while the patient was lying down on a hard surface.

Attendant Stephens was recalled. He said there were fifty-one patients in Ward 5 and four attendants in the ward on the Monday morning. There were between twenty-six and twenty-eight patients in the day room. Hawkins would have been relieved by another attendant in the day room for ten to fifteen minutes, so he could go and get some breakfast. On that morning, Hawkins was relieved by attendant Camm at twenty-five minutes to nine.

William Hawkins gave more evidence, and said that when he fetched Stephens to look at Partridge and was told to go and fetch attendant Dent, he couldn't find him. He was only away from the day room for about two minutes. He did lose sight of Partridge earlier in the morning, when he popped out of the day room to fetch water to wash other patients. This was before the patients had been served breakfast.

A few minutes before he fetched Stephens on Monday morning, he had noticed that Partridge's hands were dirty and went to get water, but he was only away for a minute. About ten minutes after washing Partridge's hands, he noticed a gurgling sound in his throat, but didn't worry about it because he had heard him make this noise before. Ten minutes after that, he saw that Partridge's head was hanging down to one side, and it was then that he went to fetch Stephens.

The Coroner then warned Hawkins that he did not have to answer the questions he was about to ask him, and cautioned him against saying anything to incriminate himself. In reply to his questions, Hawkins said that he did not, on that Monday or on any other day, use violence of any kind towards Partridge, except to lay hold of his collar or his arm to lead him away, and this was never done in an angry or violent manner. Sometimes Partridge had refused to get in or out of the bath, but not on this particular Monday. When it had happened on other occasions, Hawkins had called for assistance.

Hawkins stated that nothing had come to his knowledge regarding how Partridge had come by his injuries, except that he had been told by some patients and attendant Jennings that on Sunday Partridge had fallen by the pump-house when breaking windows. He understood that he had fallen into some bushes, and Jennings and a patient called Reason had helped him up.

On Monday morning, Partridge was quieter than usual. The bathroom door was open at all times when an attendant was inside with a patient. Stephens was going backwards and forwards past the door. He was in the bathroom with Partridge for ten or twelve minutes. When he later went out of the day room for a minute or two, there was no attendant, which was against the rules. On his return, he didn't notice anything wrong with Partridge.

In reply to a question asked by Dr Thomas, Hawkins said, 'I asked if the deceased's body had slipped out of the hands of the attendants carrying it, in taking it out of the coffin on to the slab at the mortuary.'

This part of the inquiry lasted five hours. The hearing was then adjourned for another week.

On Monday, 26 June, the inquest resumed. Samuel Hopkins, an attendant who had helped Stephens to lay out Partridge's body, was questioned. He had first seen Partridge that Monday at a quarter to eight, when he was sitting at the breakfast table waiting for his food. He didn't see him again until about ten minutes to ten, when Partridge appeared to be dying. Hopkins and Stephens had washed Partridge's body at about half past eleven in the morning. The body was afterwards taken downstairs and placed in a coffin. They had to carry the body down twelve to fifteen steps, but at no time had they let it fall.

Attendant Stephens was questioned next and stated that an hour or two after hearing about Partridge's injuries, he asked Hawkins if he knew anything about it, and he said he did not. He had spoken to him several times since, and on one occasion Hawkins had told him about Partridge falling in the day room on the Sunday afternoon.

Attendants Knight and Moulder, who had helped take Partridge's body to the mortuary, were asked whether the body had fallen while it was being conveyed. The two men emphatically denied this.

The foreman of the jury, Mr Matthews, said there was a rumour current in the city that thirteen of the attendants had, since the opening of the inquiry, received notice to leave. When asked if this was true, Toller replied that two of the medical assistants were about to leave, and four of the attendants had given notice, but this had nothing to do with the inquiry.

Head attendant Tom Dent was then called. He had seen Partridge in his bedroom at about half past six on the Monday morning, when he seemed in his usual health. He also seemed fine when Dent saw him later in the day room, where he was sitting at the breakfast table, crumbling bread between his fingers. He had endeavoured to find out how Partridge's injuries were caused, without success. He had helped lift the body out at the mortuary at five minutes to ten on Tuesday morning; the body had been lifted gently.

The Coroner again tried to interview several patients, but their answers to his questions were not of any help. He decided to ask for the view of an independent medical man, and to report the case to the Commissioners of Lunacy. After another gruelling session of over six hours, the inquest was adjourned for a fortnight.

The inquiry was resumed once more on Monday, 10 July. Dr G.R. Cubitt, a surgeon in Stroud, attended to give evidence as an independent medical expert, but Mr Toller was ill and unable to attend.

Before the evidence was heard, the foreman of the jury said he had to mention something which had happened the other day. One of the jurors, Mr Smith, was walking down the street when he met a group of

Postcard of the Cross, from Southgate Street, around 1910. (Author's collection)

men standing together at the Cross, one of whom was attendant William Hawkins. When Smith got near the men, Hawkins remarked, 'Here is one of the ********.' He believed three men had been present, and Mr Smith was sure it was Hawkins who had made the remark. The foreman said that it was an unpleasant enough thing to be a jury member on this case, without being insulted in the streets.

The Coroner called Hawkins and Hopkins in and asked them about the incident. Hawkins denied having made any such remark, and Hopkins said he didn't know anything about it. Mr Smith said he was sure it was Hawkins who spoke. The two attendants were allowed to stand down.

Dr G.R. Cubitt said he didn't believe that Partridge could have suffered his injuries before he was woken on Monday morning and then have got in and out of the bath without assistance, dressed himself and walked to the day room. He thought the injuries must have been inflicted after a quarter to eight on Monday morning, when Partridge was sitting in the day room. He couldn't believe that a fall in the airing yard, which was said to have happened on Sunday, or the fall in the day room on the same day, could have caused the injuries.

Tom Dent, the head attendant, was called and asked if the rumour was true that he was going to leave the asylum. He replied that this was correct, but his leaving had nothing to do with the case.

The Coroner then began summing up the evidence. He said that it appeared that the deceased had received his injuries some time on Monday and it seemed unlikely that the attendant Hawkins, who was with the patient for most of the day, knew nothing about how this had happened. He wasn't satisfied with the evidence given by Hawkins, and he thought it was an extraordinary question which he had asked, as to whether the body might have been dropped on the way to the mortuary.

All the witnesses agreed that Partridge was in his usual health at a quarter to eight on Monday morning. The Coroner thought the injuries had been inflicted deliberately, and although there was no evidence to say by whom, he had his suspicions. The jury foreman said, 'So have we.'

The Coroner told the jury that the law provided that if a man was suffering from a disease and another man inflicted injuries upon him which accelerated his death, he was guilty of murder or manslaughter. To be manslaughter, there must be extenuating circumstances, such as a fight or a struggle. No such evidence had come forth in this case, and if they concluded that the injuries had been inflicted wilfully and maliciously, then this was a case of wilful murder.

After considering for a short time, the jury returned a verdict of wilful murder against some person or persons unknown. The Coroner commented that it was perfectly monstrous that people who were sent to that institution to be cared for and treated properly should be subjected to such terrible treatment as that poor man had received.

The foreman suggested that there should be some inquiry into the management of the asylum. He believed it was entirely owing to the many changes in staff and mismanagement of the institution that they were there that day. The Coroner replied that he was sorry that Mr Toller was not there to hear that remark, but the question raised was one for the Visiting Committee. The inquiry was then closed. The proceedings in this final session had lasted three and a half hours.

In July, it was announced in the local newspapers that the Visiting Justices (magistrates who oversaw the running of the asylum and carried out inspections) had commenced an inquiry into the circumstances of the affair. They had suspended all the attendants whose names had been called into question and placed the matter formally in the hands of the police, who were searching for additional evidence which might lead to someone standing trial. The Lunacy Commissioners (officials who addressed any issues that arose in asylums) had also started an investigation. Attendant Stephens had resigned since the inquest. Near the end of the month, it was reported that Mr Toller, the superintendent of the asylum, had sent in his resignation, because his health had given way 'under the stress of duty'.

It wasn't until November 1882 that news broke that an arrest had finally been made. Deputy Chief Constable Chipp had gone to the lodgings of William Hawkins on 3 November, at about seven o'clock in the evening, armed with a warrant which had been issued by the Treasury. Hawkins was arrested on suspicion of causing the death of Walter Partridge.

The next day, Hawkins was brought before the County Petty Sessional Court. Mr Pollard, Solicitor to the Treasury, said he appeared under instructions received from the Secretary of State for the Home Department, Sir William Vernon Harcourt. The circumstances of the case had been brought to the attention of the Home Secretary, along with the report of the Lunacy Commissioners, and he deemed it right that the prisoner should be brought before the court to decide if he should be sent for trial. Hawkins was remanded until Friday.

On Friday, 10 November, William Hawkins was brought before the county magistrates at the Grand Jury Room, in Shire Hall. A large crowd had gathered outside. Mr Pollard was there to prosecute; Mr Taynton defended the prisoner. Mr Morton York appeared on behalf of Partridge's relatives.

Key to the prosecution's case was the evidence of Henry Dyke, head night attendant at the asylum. Dyke said that on the day Partridge died,

Sir W.V. Harcourt, Home Secretary in 1882. (Author's collection)

a patient named Alfred Radbourn had told him that he saw Hawkins punch Partridge and kneel on him in the bathroom. When Dyke was asked by Mr Taynton why he hadn't mentioned this at the inquest, he said that he had only replied to specific questions, and he did not recall being asked if he had anything to add.

Alfred Radbourn, the patient who made the accusation, was put in the witness box. He said there were two attendants in the bathroom who got Partridge down on the floor and stamped on his belly. He said he had witnessed the attack as he walked up and down the corridor, passing the bathroom door.

Mr Taynton, defending the prisoner, pointed out that no one had implicated Hawkins except the poor lunatic, and Hawkins could not have attacked Partridge in the bathroom because several witnesses saw Partridge walk freely to the day room and later eat his breakfast.

The magistrates retired to consider the evidence, and on their return announced their intention to commit the prisoner to stand trial at the next assizes on a charge of manslaughter. Hawkins was granted bail.

Three months later, on 15 February 1883, the trial of William Hawkins began before Judge Baron Huddleston. Hawkins, who was thirty-eight years old and now described as a labourer, was charged with feloniously killing and slaying Walter Partridge at the County Lunatic Asylum, Gloucester, on 12 June 1882. The prisoner pleaded not guilty.

Mr Lawrence opened the case for the prosecution and started by commenting that there were obvious difficulties in getting evidence in cases of this kind, because it could only be obtained from two sources – the attendants, who were companions of the accused and were, naturally, reluctant to incriminate one of their own, and the patients, whose evidence had to be treated with caution.

Baron Huddleston, in *The Graphic*, 3 July 1875. (Author's collection)

However, the matter must be sifted to the bottom, because it was of vital importance to the State that helpless inmates of asylums should not be subject to injuries which led to their deaths.

Thomas Dancey, the tailor who also acted as a part-time attendant, gave his evidence next. Cross-examined by the counsel for the defence, Dancey said that forty or fifty attendants in total were employed at the asylum. About fifty prisoners were in the yard on Sunday, 11 June, and there were only two attendants on duty. The patients frequently quarrelled and knocked each other down, but he hadn't seen any patient attacking Partridge on that morning.

Henry Howard, shoemaker at the asylum, was another part-time attendant who had also been in the airing yard on that Sunday, between half past ten and twelve o'clock. He saw Partridge breaking some glass in the pump-house with slates from the roof. Howard had struggled to get a slate from him and Partridge fell backwards into the shrubbery. Later, Partridge had an altercation with a patient named Wilkins, but he didn't see Wilkins strike Partridge. Howard had got hold of Partridge to break up the tussle and fell over backwards, and Partridge landed on top of him. He got up and gave Partridge into the custody of Dancey. Howard later saw Partridge at dinner but didn't notice anything the matter with him.

William Jennings, formerly an attendant, said he was on duty on Sunday, 11 June, and Partridge was in his care in the afternoon from three o'clock till half past three; he saw him again just before four o'clock. Partridge seemed to be in his usual health. Another attendant named Vick said he saw Partridge on Sunday, at half past three in the afternoon and again a little after four o'clock, and Partridge seemed to be fine. Cross-examined, he said there were generally six attendants in Ward 5, but they were rather short-handed at that time.

Attendant Henry Dyke said that he saw Partridge on Sunday, 11 June at about a quarter past eleven at night. He was quiet in bed. He checked on him from time to time during the night and each time Partridge was asleep. He saw him at half past five the next morning, awake. He seemed in his usual state of health and said, 'Good morning'. Dyke went off duty at six and the day attendants, Stephens, Hawkins and Hopkins took over. Dyke was on duty again from two o'clock on Monday, the day Partridge had died. In the airing yard, the patient, Radbourn, said something to him about Partridge's death. On the following night, he asked Hawkins whether he had a struggle with Partridge and he denied it. Dyke told Hawkins that Radbourn had said he had a struggle with Partridge and got him down and knelt on him, then thumped him in the stomach. Hawkins said this had not happened; Partridge bathed and dressed, and then Hawkins took him to the day room.

Cross-examined, Dyke said he hadn't revealed this at the Coroner's inquest, but only answered the questions he was asked. He didn't volunteer the statement because the patients were in the habit of making unfounded charges against those who were most kind to them. Radbourn was subject to fits, and when he came round didn't know what he was doing. Dyke had known Hawkins for two years. He was good-tempered and kind, and the last person in the world to harm anyone under his charge. Re-examined by the prosecution, Dyke said he didn't know whether Radbourn had had a fit that morning. In answer to a question from the judge, he said Radbourn was subject to delusions. The judge remarked that he thought Radbourn was an unreliable witness.

Mr Coren, the Coroner, said that he commenced the inquest into the death of Walter Partridge on 14 June 1882. The deposition of Hawkins was read out, in which he denied any knowledge of how the deceased's injuries were inflicted. Coren revealed that there had been another inquest at the asylum since that on Partridge. A man had died after receiving injuries to his ribs, but no blame was attached to the attendants in that case.

Frederick Charles Stephens, now a former attendant, once again gave his evidence concerning what had happened in the hours before Partridge died. Cross-examined, Stephens said he was not hard of hearing, and the bathroom door had been open all the time Hawkins and Partridge were in there. He would have heard any struggle. Three other attendants who were also in the dormitory didn't hear anything either. Hawkins was kind to the patients and Partridge was fond of him.

Samuel Hopkins, former attendant, said on 11 June that he and Hawkins were the only attendants on duty in Ward 5 in the afternoon. The next morning, he saw Partridge at the breakfast table and there seemed nothing wrong with him. He saw him next sitting on a locker, when he was dying.

Attendant Albert Camm said he went on duty at six in the morning on 12 June. He relieved Hawkins in the day room at half past eight. Hawkins was away for twenty minutes. Partridge seemed in good health.

Tom Dent, late head attendant, gave the same evidence as he had at the inquest. Cross-examined, he said he had asked Hawkins if he had struggled with Partridge in the bathroom and Hawkins said he hadn't.

Alfred Radbourn, whose evidence was key to the prosecution's case, was then called. He said he had been an inmate at the asylum for twenty-one years. His father had told him he was nearly thirty-two. He remembered Partridge and on the morning in question he had seen him with Hawkins in the dormitory. Partridge was handled roughly by Hawkins and two or three others. They got hold of him by the neck and nearly choked him. Asked what he thought of the accused, he said, 'I never knew a better man than Hawkins'. The judge asked him where Partridge was when the attendants got him down and he replied that he was in the bath. They had pulled him from the dormitory into the bathroom. They got him down on the boards, pulled his shirt off and kicked him about, then got him against the bath. Then they got on him again and handled him roughly, kicking and thumping him. Radbourn told the court that Hawkins was the roughest; he didn't like Hawkins at all.

Questioned some more, Radbourn next said that Hawkins was 'the honestest man he ever clapped eyes on'. He was always very kind and he had never fallen out with him. Dent was then put in the witness box beside the witness, who was asked if this was one of the men he saw assaulting Partridge. Radbourn replied that he was. The same exercise was carried out with Camm ('No'), Hopkins ('Present but didn't take part'), Camm again ('Hit Partridge once or twice'), Stephens ('Yes'), Dyke ('No'), and Bick ('No').

Mr Toller then gave his evidence. He believed the injuries to the ribs might have been caused on the Sunday before Partridge died. His (Partridge's) friends had visited him on Saturday and thought he was dying then. His bones would have been very brittle, because he was a paralytic, and he wouldn't suffer as much pain as another person.

The judge then asked the prosecution if there was any point in continuing, as their case depended on the evidence of 'that unhappy lunatic'.

Gloucester Asylum, in *Six Engravings of Public Buildings in the City of Gloucester* by A.N. Smith. (Gloucestershire Archives, D9795/2/4/5)

Partridge could have received his injuries on the Sunday, when he was got hold of round the ribs, and he wouldn't have betrayed any indication of pain. Mr Lawrence said other doctors aside from Mr Toller believed the injuries were inflicted much nearer the time of death, but he would agree to go no further with the prosecution.

The jury then considered their verdict and found William Hawkins not guilty. The mystery of how Walter Partridge's ribs were broken remains unsolved.

'WILL YOU COME DOWNSTAIRS AND SEE TO YOUR WIFE, FOR YOU HAVE KILLED HER'

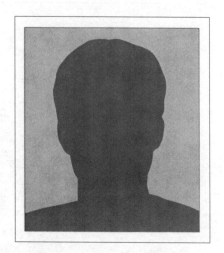

Suspect: Edward Hewett
Age: Thirty-four
Charge: Murder

On 5 January 1885, a marriage took place at St Mark's parish church in Worcester Street, Kingsholm. The groom was Edward Hewett, aged thirty-three and a boiler-maker by trade, who had moved to Gloucester from his home town of Loughborough, in Leicestershire. His bride was Sarah Ann Reed, aged thirty-nine, who was a widow. One of the witnesses was Sarah's brother, William Chamberlain.

Sarah's first husband had been John Reed, who worked for the Gloucester company of Fielding and Platt, at the Atlas Iron Works. They had married in 1864 and had four children. In 1878, John was sent by his employers to Rochester in Kent, where he was engaged in helping to build an iron chimney for a company there. In January 1879, it was announced that John had been killed accidentally, when he suffocated in a flue connected with the new chimney. Fielding and Platt paid the funeral expenses, and for a time also paid Sarah Reed a small allowance.

St Mark's parish church, Kingsholm. (Author's collection)

Some time after she was widowed, Sarah started a relationship with Edward Hewett, and in 1882 they had a child, whose birth was registered with the name Edward Hewett Reed. Another child, Samuel James Hewett, was born late in 1885, but he only lived for a few months.

Edward and Sarah Hewett lived at 2 Wells Court, off Sherborne Street. Wells Court contained a group of tightly packed houses, which shared a wash house in the yard. The walls of the houses were only one-brick thick, and all the occupants could hear what was happening in each other's homes. It soon became clear to the Hewetts' neighbours that the couple had a difficult marriage. Edward Hewett had a nasty temper when he was drunk and Sarah could often be heard crying out, but would tolerate no interference from the neighbours or from the police.

Although Edward Hewett was a trained boiler-maker, he did not have a permanent job, and often had to leave Gloucester in search of work. In April 1886, Hewett was employed for a week at Sharpness Point. He returned home on Saturday, 17 April, at about three o'clock in the afternoon.

Mrs Emily Curtis lived next door to the couple and soon after Hewett got home, Sarah came round and showed her a sovereign which her husband had just given her, then went out to get him something for his tea. Soon after she returned, Mrs Curtis heard Sarah cry, 'Don't strike me, Ted! What have I done? Don't be foolish.' She told him she had got him some bacon and eggs for his tea. Then there was a loud crash and Mrs Curtis heard Hewett swearing at his wife, followed by one or two blows, and Sarah screamed, 'Murder!' The disturbance lasted about twenty minutes, then Mrs Curtis heard Sarah say, 'For God's sake, Ted, don't hit me any more, you'll kill me. You murder-wife!'

Previously, Sarah had warned her neighbour never to interfere unless she was called. On this occasion she called out several times for help. Mrs Curtis went to the house and was met in the doorway by Hewett, who lifted up his fist in a threatening manner and asked what she wanted. She replied quietly, 'Hello Teddy, what you come back safe.' Sarah Hewett cried, 'I will insist on you coming in to me, Mrs Curtis!' Hewett walked up to the fireplace and she went in. Sarah was crouching on the ground between two chairs, and said, 'He's murdering me.' Hewett said that she had claimed that she had suffered a miscarriage, and moved towards his wife to kick her, but Mrs Curtis prevented him by putting her arm across his chest and pushing him back. Hewett said something else about a supposed miscarriage and threatened that if his wife was lying, he would kick the baby out of her.

After everything had finally calmed down, Mrs Curtis left and all was quiet for a while, but at about five o'clock she heard another altercation. She went round again, but this time found the door was locked. Later, she heard Hewett go out, and she took Sarah a cup of tea.

Between three and four o'clock the following morning, screams of 'Murder!' and blows were heard from the Hewett's bedroom by the neighbours who lived either side of their house; Mrs Curtis on one side, and Thomas Knight on the other. The argument appeared to be about money, because Hewett shouted, 'I want that six shillings', and his wife said, 'I shall not give it to you, Ted, for I haven't got it.' He threatened to hit her eye out if she didn't give him the money. Then a heavy thud was heard, as if someone had fallen on the bedroom floor.

At half past eight on Sunday morning, Sarah came round to Mrs Curtis and showed her the bruises on her forehead and chin. Later that morning, at about half past eleven, Hewett was heard shouting at his wife, and then he went out.

At around three in the afternoon, Mrs Curtis heard Hewett demand his dinner, and his wife replied that there was a nice dinner ready for him. He objected to eating such 'tack'. Soon after, Sarah ran out into the court, screaming, 'You're a murder-wife!' Hewett followed, hurling abuse and threats.

Thomas Knight was standing outside his door and saw Hewett chase his wife into the wash house, throw her down and kick her. Soon after that, Sarah went to Mrs Curtis's window, with tears pouring down her cheeks and a death-struck look on her face. She said, 'Oh, Mrs Curtis, let me die in your house.' Her neighbour took Sarah back to her own house and made her a cup of tea, but she could only drink a little. She put a linseed poultice on the distraught woman's stomach, then returned home.

At about six o'clock that evening, there was a tapping on the wall between the two houses and Mrs Curtis went next door, where she found Sidney Reed, Sarah's eldest boy, supporting his mother as she sat on a chair. Various other female neighbours were already there, gathered round. Some brandy was fetched from the nearby White Lion Inn and Mrs Curtis and the other women tried to give her some, but she couldn't take it. Later that evening, Sarah Hewett died.

On Monday, 19 April 1886, Edward Hewett was brought before the magistrates at Shire Hall, for a preliminary hearing. News of the death of Sarah Ann Hewett had already spread around Gloucester, and the Bearland entrance to the court was crowded with people when the prisoner was brought in.

Hewett was described by watching reporters as being 'an unkempt, determined-looking individual'. Deputy Chief Constable Chipp said that Wells Court contained fourteen or fifteen houses, occupied by 'persons in humble circumstances in life'. He had come across Mrs Hewett before, because about a month previously she had come to the court while her husband was away looking for work, and asked for relief towards the cost of burying her child, who was lying dead at home. The magistrates had ordered him to give her money from the Poor Box.

Mr Chipp outlined the case briefly, saying that in the previous week, Edward Hewett had been away working at Sharpness, and on his return home he had given his wife a sovereign but later demanded six shillings back, which she refused to give him. This had led to several outbreaks of violence over Saturday and Sunday, and Mrs Hewett had died on Sunday evening. Hewett was remanded while further investigations were carried out.

On Monday night, an inquest was opened at the White Lion Inn, on the corner of Sherborne Street and Alvin Street. The members of the jury had to walk through a narrow passage to reach Wells Court, where they viewed Sarah Hewett's body. It was, said a reporter, 'a miserable business, the court being dark, the cottage small and squalid, and the crowd outside exhibiting a morbid curiosity into all that was going on.' After viewing the body, the Coroner and jury made their way to the police court, and began to hear the evidence.

The first witness was Sarah Hewett's brother, William Chamberlain, who had been the witness at her wedding. He said he lived near his sister, at 3 Powells Passage, Sweetbriar Street, but he hadn't seen her for about a fortnight, until he went to the house to identify her body. He didn't know whether she had lived on good terms with her husband, because he had never visited her house.

Lucy Howell of 19 Sherborne Street, said that on Saturday night, between seven and eight o'clock, she had seen the Hewetts near the White

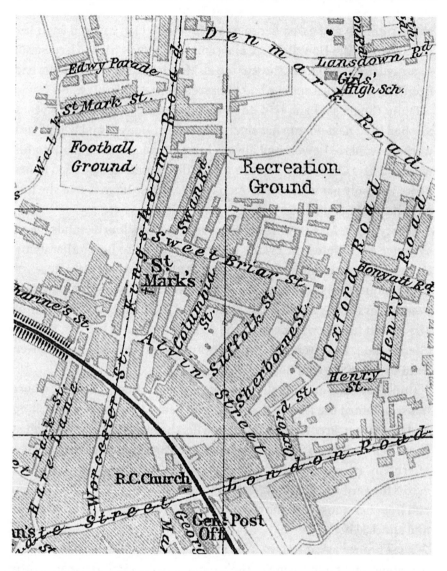

Detail from Baedeker's map, 1910, showing the Sherborne Street area. (Author's collection)

Lion Inn. She saw Hewett strike his wife in the face, then he had kicked her on the hip and swore at her. He was angry, but Mrs Howell couldn't say if he had been drinking.

On Sunday night, at about six o'clock, Mrs Howell went to their house and found Sarah sitting in a chair. Sarah told her that Hewett had hit her in the stomach and asked her to go to the White Lion Inn and fetch her some brandy. Mrs Howell did so, and some neighbours tried to feed Sarah some with a teaspoon, but she was too ill. Mrs Howell said the Hewetts had frequently quarrelled and she had often seen Hewett strike his wife.

Emily Curtis said she had known Mrs Hewett for five or six years. She had lived next door to her since she married Hewett, and was a hard-working woman. Hewett had always been a 'bad, drinking man' to his wife, and Mrs Curtis didn't like to repeat the expressions he used to her. There was only a one-brick partition between their houses, and she had often heard the couple quarrelling.

Sidney Reed, Mrs Hewett's eldest son, who was fourteen, also gave evidence and related the events which had led up to his mother dying. He stated that he had often seen his stepfather kick and beat his mother.

The inquest was adjourned for two days. In the meantime, the local newspapers reported that Mr Chipp had said that the children of Mrs Hewett had been taken in by the deceased woman's brother, William Chamberlain. They were in a 'sadly destitute condition', and he had given them £1 out of the Poor Box.

On Wednesday evening the inquest resumed. Thomas Knight, whose house adjoined the Hewetts', said he had heard the couple quarrelling, and Hewett apparently attacking his wife, through his bedroom wall at about four o'clock on Sunday morning. At about three o'clock on Sunday afternoon, he was standing on his doorstep, from where he could see across the yard and under the door of the wash house. He saw Mrs Hewett run from her house into the wash house, and her husband ran after her and attacked her.

The Coroner asked Knight if he meant to say that he had stood there watching, and hadn't gone to the woman's assistance. Members of the jury muttered, 'Hear, hear'. Didn't it occur to him to go to her assistance? Knight said he did not know, he thought it better to keep away from Hewett. The Coroner replied that he could not understand any Englishman standing by and seeing that. 'However, that is the explanation you give, and I think it is most disgraceful.' Knight was then asked if he had told anyone else what was happening, to which Knight replied that he hadn't. Asked if anyone else was about at the time, he said, 'I saw a neighbour standing against the door, that is all.' When asked by the Coroner if a cry of murder was such a normal thing there that he took no notice of it, Knight replied that he had only been living at Wells Court for two or three weeks.

Summing up, the Coroner said it was understandable that Mrs Hewett had not wanted to give up the six shillings to her husband, considering that she had had to beg for money to bury a child only a few weeks before. However, he had to say in fairness to Hewett that it must be acknowledged that he had met with 'a certain amount of trumpery provocation' from his wife. A juryman protested, saying, 'Not at all, I think.' The Coroner continued on, saying that the money had belonged to the man and he had a right to demand it by proper means, but of course the provocation was too slight to justify murder.

The jury returned a verdict that Sarah Ann Hewett had been wilfully murdered by Edward Hewett.

A week after his first appearance in court, on Monday, 28 April, Hewett was brought before the mayor and two other magistrates at the City Police Court. Deputy Chief Constable Mr Chipp said that since Hewett's remand, the whole case had been laid before the Solicitor of the Treasury, and he asked the Bench to commit the prisoner for trial on the capital charge of wilful murder. After giving the magistrates some background details about the case, Mr Chipp produced Hewett's hobnailed boots, which he said the prisoner had used to kick his wife. This created a sensation in the court.

William Chamberlain, Lucy Howell and Emily Curtis all repeated the evidence they had given at the inquest, then Sidney Reed gave a fuller account of what he had seen on that afternoon.

On Sunday afternoon, he came home from Sunday school and found his mother and stepfather arguing. Hewett called his mother an old cow and threatened to knock her over if she did not find him some money. She ran out across the court and went in to the wash house, where she hid her purse behind the tap. Hewett followed her into the wash house and demanded the money. He flung her down on the ground and kicked her in the stomach twice. She got up and Hewett caught sight of the purse. She tried to drag him back to prevent him from getting it, but he grabbed the purse and knocked her down, kicking her again. She said nothing, but walked back into the house, and Hewett came indoors.

Hewett went upstairs and while he was there, a neighbour, Mrs Cooke, came in and called up to him, saying he should come down because his wife was dying. Hewett replied that she was just drunk and they should throw a bucket of water over her. He took some money out of the purse, then put on his hat and left, taking his three-year-old son with him.

The neighbours went away and Sidney attended his mother. He put her in a chair first, then on the floor by the fire. She kissed him and told him to give her love to his brothers and sisters. Then he knocked on the wall and Mrs Curtis and some other women came in, and they tried to give her some brandy, but she couldn't drink it. She then died.

The boy was then questioned by Hewett, who was defending himself. Asked if he had seen Hewett take money out of the purse, he replied that he had, and he also saw him pick some money off the floor. Hewett asked him if the money had not dropped out of his mother's bosom, and he said it hadn't. His mother had tried to stop Hewett from getting it from behind the tap. 'And wasn't that when she fell down?' Hewett asked. Sidney answered, 'You knocked her down and kicked her twice in the chest.'

Thomas Knight was next to appear and related what he had seen on the Sunday afternoon, when he was standing outside his door. He said he saw Mrs Hewett come out of her house and go into the wash house through the broken end of the wall. She was running and her husband ran after her. In the wash house, Hewett struck her and she fell down. He then kicked her in the small of the back. She was lying against the door, which was broken at the bottom, and he could see underneath. They were in there for about five minutes then returned to the house, the prisoner going in first. The witness heard him say to his wife, 'I gave you some money, and you hided it in your bosom.'

Questioned by the prisoner, Knight said he saw him knock Mrs Hewett down; he didn't see him take money off the floor, he didn't see the deceased pulling him, and he didn't see her pick up half a brick.

Clara Cooke, wife of William Cooke, of 14 Sherborne Street, had known the prisoner for about fifteen months, and knew Sarah Hewett before her marriage. She went to the house on Sunday, at about half past three in the afternoon, where she found her neighbour exhausted, her head hanging over the back of her chair. She had bruises on her forehead and under her jaw. Mrs Cooke went to the foot of the stairs and called up, 'If you please, Mr Hewett, will you come downstairs and see to your wife, for you have killed her.' He came down and said they should let her die, and to fetch a bucket of water and throw it over her. Mrs Cooke told him, 'You will have to pay for all you are saying, and all you are doing.' He shook some money in his hand and said, 'Now I'm off. I've got to work for my money, not to put it behind the tap. This is to pay for my train fare, and this ****** is off.' His language was so foul that Mrs Cooke left the house. At about six o'clock she returned, but Hewett was not there. Mrs Hewett was partly sitting on a chair and partly on the floor. Mrs Curtis got her into an armchair and tried to give her some brandy. She died about seven o'clock. She believed the deceased was perfectly sober.

In answer to the prisoner's questions, she said that he didn't say that he had seen his wife in a drunken fit before, and he didn't say to his son, 'Come on, Ted, we will have a walk while she gets sober.'

Police Constable Gobey said that on that Sunday night, he was called to Sherborne Street at about a quarter past seven. He saw Mrs Hewett sitting in an armchair in the kitchen, with two or three females attending her. She was breathing hard and appeared to be dying. He went to fetch Mr Hepworth, the police surgeon, who came back to the house with him. When they got there, the woman was dead. Shortly after, he met the prisoner in Sherborne Street and told him he wanted him. Hewett asked what for, and Gobey said he would know why when they got to the police station. At the station the prisoner was searched, and was found to have on him nine shillings and sixpence.

George Hepworth, the surgeon, said he was summoned to the prisoner's house on the Sunday evening, where he found Mrs Hewett had recently died. The following day he carried out a post-mortem. The body exhibited sundry marks of violence; there were many bruises on the body, including two large ones over her right buttock and hip, with indentations of hobnails. The bruise on the temple was a very severe one, with the underlying muscle reduced to pulp. There was also deep bruising to the stomach, which contained a considerable amount of food, but there was no odour of alcohol. All the organs were healthy. He believed death was caused by shock to the nervous system, consequent upon the severe injuries she had received, and more particularly the blow to the stomach.

Hewett was then formally charged with the murder of Sarah Ann Hewett. In response he said, 'All I can say is I was drunk and know nothing about it.' He was committed to take his trial at Worcester Assizes in May.

On Monday, 24 May, the trial of Edward Hewett began at Worcester Shire Hall, before Mr Justice Stephen. Females and juvenile spectators were excluded from the court because of the excessive amount of foul language which the witnesses were obliged to use, in repeating what they had heard the prisoner saying. Hewett, who appeared to be ill, sat on a seat in the dock. Mr Fitzroy Cowper opened the case for the prosecution, and spoke at great length. He said the evidence was of a most revolting character and the treatment the prisoner had given his wife was exceedingly distressing and brutal.

William Chamberlain gave his evidence, as he had at the inquest and magistrates' hearing. Cross-examined, he said that his sister and her husband had been very poor, and in the winter Hewett had been out of work a great deal. Sidney Reed then gave his evidence, and told the court that it was his fifteenth birthday.

Details were given at the trial which revealed some of Hewett's movements when he left the house on the Sunday, before and after his final attacks on his

Shire Hall, Worcester. (Author's collection)

wife. At about half past twelve, he had gone to the house of his sister-in-law, Emma Curtis, who lived in St Mary's Square. He paid for three quarts of beer, which were drunk by himself, Emma Curtis and her husband, and Mr Cleveley, his brother-in-law. He was invited to stay for supper, but declined and went home. After attacking his wife in the wash house, Hewett left with his son to go to the Wellington Hotel, next to the railway station. He had a drink and asked about the time of the train to Normanton, a junction for Loughborough. On finding he had missed the train, he headed home with his son and was arrested when he got to Sherborne Street.

The police surgeon gave his evidence concerning the post-mortem. Cross-examined by the counsel for the defence, he said the injury to the deceased woman's left temple might have been caused by her falling on some loose bricks in the wash house. He also agreed with the defence counsel that 'bad spirits', taken by someone who had suffered privation, might make a man not master of his own actions.

Mr Cowper, in addressing the jury, said four distinct attacks on Mrs Hewett over the weekend had been proved. There could be no doubt that she had died through the maltreatment of the prisoner, and there was nothing in the

The Wellington Hotel, near the railway station. (Author's collection)

circumstances which would justify the jury in returning any verdict except that of wilful murder.

Mr Jackson, the defence lawyer, asked the jury to find the prisoner guilty of manslaughter, because all the evidence pointed to the theory that he was not responsible for his actions at the time. Mr Jackson suggested that the prisoner had received provocation, through the refusal of his wife to give him the money he demanded. Her opposition heated and excited him and led him to inflict blows which he would never otherwise have inflicted. He went on to claim that the prisoner could never have imagined that his blows would result in her death.

Judge Stephen, in summing up the case for the jury, said the idea that the prisoner had received provocation which justified the use of any violence was absurd. The woman had only done what she conceived to be her duty as a wife, in refusing to let him squander in drink the money he had given her. He went on to explain that in English law, if a man intentionally inflicted grievous bodily harm and his victim died as a result, that was murder. It made no difference if he had not intended to kill, nor if he had been drunk. If the jury thought that Edward Hewett caused this woman's death by means which showed an intention to do her grievous bodily harm, then being drunk would not absolve him. If they thought he 'knocked her about' without knowing what he did or meant, then they could find him guilty of manslaughter.

The jury retired for fifteen minutes before returning with a verdict of guilty of murder, but recommended mercy because there had been no premeditation. The judge then addressed Hewett, telling him he had used cruel,

Sir J.F. Stephen (Mr Justice Stephen), in the *Illustrated London News*, 15 February 1879. (Author's collection)

repeated and prolonged violence towards his wife. He then sentenced Hewett to death. He was returned to Gloucester Prison, where his execution was to take place.

On 12 June, *The Citizen* reported that the Home Secretary had informed Gloucester City's High Sheriff that Edward Hewett was not going to be reprieved. The report also said that it had emerged that the deceased woman had not been legally married to her second husband, because Hewett had a wife still living in Loughborough.

On the following day, which was a Sunday, an open-air religious service was held in the vicinity of Wells Court, attended by 200-300 local people. The service was arranged by the vicar of St Mark's Church, the Reverend Bartlett. As well as mourning the death of Sarah Ann Hewett, the crowd was asked to pray for the condemned man.

On the morning of Tuesday, 15 June 1886, the execution of Edward Hewett took place. Hewett had been visited by his mother before his condemnation and by his father after his fate was confirmed. He was also visited

Hangman James Berry. (Author's collection)

by his sisters-in-law, Mrs Emma Curtis and Mrs Cleveley. He had expressed penitence and regret for his crime, but said he had not had any intention of murdering his wife.

Executions at one time had taken place on the prison gatehouse roof, but now were held behind the walls, in one of the yards. The hangman was James Berry, who inspected the scaffold before Hewett was brought out of the condemned cell at eight o'clock. Hewett looked dazed, and if he had glanced to one side he would have seen an open grave waiting to receive his body. As Berry adjusted the noose, Hewett was heard to say, 'Oh dear.' Berry quickly drew the bolt to open the trapdoors, and Hewett disappeared from view. Unfortunately, the hangman must have made a miscalculation in deciding how much rope would be needed, because when the prison doctor examined the body, he estimated that it had taken Hewett at least two minutes to die. After the obligatory post-mortem was conducted, a notice was pinned to the prison gates declaring that the execution of Edward Hewett had taken place.

After giving an account of the execution, *The Citizen* gave more details about Hewett's past. Born in Loughborough in 1852, he had married a girl there called Eliza Wooddale when he was twenty

Gloucester Prison's gates, on which a notice confirming Hewett's execution was placed. (Jill Evans)

years old, and they had two children. After a few years, the couple separated and Hewett's wife had moved in with another man, and had four children by him. Hewett had come to Gloucester five or six years ago, and met the widowed Sarah Ann Reed. When she married Hewett in 1885, she believed him to be single. She found out that Hewett's first wife was still alive when his mother visited from Loughborough.

The five orphaned children of Mrs Hewett had not been sent to the work-house, but were being cared for by Sarah's brother and sisters. The police had said that Sidney Reed 'had made a good deal of capital of the fact that he is connected with the now notorious family'.

CASE FIVE 1903

'IN GREAT MENTAL TROUBLE'

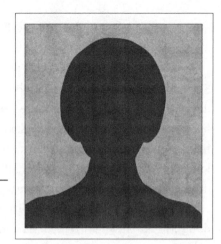

Suspect: Agnes Mould
Age: Thirty-eight
Charge: Murder

On 21 May 1903, an inquest was opened at the Lower George Hotel in Westgate Street. The City Coroner, Charles Scott, told the inquest jury that they were investigating the death of a three-week-old baby, who had died two days previously. The infant's mother, Mrs Agnes Mould, had been admitted to the Gloucester County Lunatic Asylum and was too ill to attend the hearing.

The first witness was the child's father, tailor William Mould of 156 High Street, Tredworth, who was also the landlord of the Duke of Wellington public house in Tredworth Road. He told the inquest that the baby, a girl, had been born on 27 April. His wife had been in good health physically before her confinement, but she was rather low and depressed, and complained of pains in her head. A week before she went into labour, she had tied a handkerchief once or twice around her neck, he thought in an endeavour to 'do away with herself'. She had also thrown one of her four children out of a window. After the birth, his wife was still depressed, and the baby was kept from her at first on the advice of the doctor, but then she improved and the baby was entrusted to her.

On 11 May, his wife was sent to stay with her mother, in the hope that a change of scene would help to lift her spirits. Mould visited her there a few times, and she seemed a lot better in health and mind. However, he was sent for on 19 May, and was told the baby was dead. His wife was crying and upset, but she said nothing to him about how the baby had died. Later, she told the doctor that she had pressed the child to her breast and that had killed it. On 20 May, his wife was committed to the County Asylum at Wotton.

Agnes Mould's mother, Mrs Eliza Pollard, lived at 51 Seymour Road. She told the inquest that her daughter was in a bad mental state both on the day of the birth and on the day after. She was quieter on the third day, and the baby was brought to her. She seemed very fond of it and fed it naturally. When her daughter was brought to stay at her house, she was very poorly and very low. Mrs Pollard slept with her daughter and the baby, and saw her frequently during the day. She didn't ever leave them alone for long.

On Tuesday, 19 May, she got up as usual at five o'clock, leaving her daughter and the baby in bed. At a quarter to six, she took her daughter a cup of tea and an egg, and was in and out of the room several times before breakfast. At about a quarter to ten, she went upstairs and her daughter was feeding the baby. Agnes said the child had a stomach ache and that she was very tired and wanted to go to sleep. She was lying on her right side with her child at her right breast. Mrs Pollard pulled down the bedclothes and checked the baby was all right, then she went back downstairs.

All was quiet for about twenty minutes, until her daughter came down to the kitchen. She had her dress on, and her expression made Mrs Pollard feel frightened. Agnes said in a hurried way, 'I have done something,' and Mrs Pollard rushed upstairs, where she found the baby in the bed, in the same place she had last seen her. She looked as if she was asleep, but didn't appear to be breathing, and so Mrs Pollard blew in her nostrils to try to make her breathe. She then ran downstairs with the infant and called out to a neighbour opposite, who came at once and looked at the baby, before saying, 'It's dead.' Mrs Pollard questioned her daughter as to what had happened, but could get nothing out of her. She sent for William Mould, Dr Bibby and a policeman. Her daughter was crying and depressed all day after and she had to watch her all night and the following day, up to the time she was taken to the asylum. Between one and two o'clock, Dr Bibby, the Relieving Officer and a magistrate came, and her daughter was removed as 'a lunatic not under proper control'.

Dr Bibby said he had attended Mrs Mould for several weeks, and was called by her husband to examine her as to her mental condition. She seemed to be suffering from acute depression. Dr Bibby was not engaged to attend her at her confinement, but he saw her on the day she gave birth, in the evening. He advised that the baby be kept away from her for a day or two, as her mental health had declined since he had last seen her. He visited her almost daily for about a week, and she improved considerably under treat-

'a lunatic not under proper control'

ment. The baby was returned to her under his sanction. He didn't see her again until 9 May, when she was very bad again mentally – more depressed and melancholy than ever, and crying bitterly, as if in great grief and trouble. It was then that he first advised her husband to make a formal application for her removal to the asylum.

When Dr Bibby was called on 19 May, the child was dead, but there was nothing obvious to say what had been the cause of death. He asked

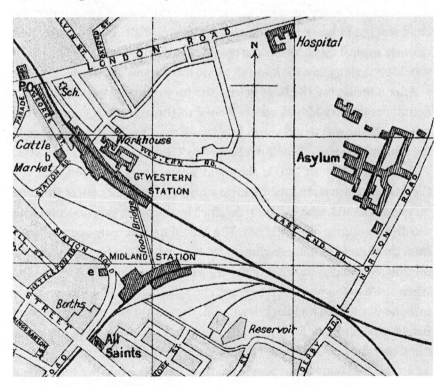

Detail from a 1924 map showing the asylum. (Author's collection)

Mrs Mould how she was getting on, then how the baby was, and finally, getting no response, he asked her if she had done anything to the baby. She gave no reply. She was taken to another room and he asked her again to tell him all about it. She replied that she did not know why she had done it. He asked her, 'What did you do?' and she said she was breastfeeding the baby and held it close to her until it could not breathe.

He saw her again on Wednesday afternoon, and she was still the same. She was undoubtedly of unsound mind and incapable of taking care of herself. The post-mortem carried out by Dr Bibby concluded that the infant had died of suffocation. This could have been caused by 'over-laying', that is by the mother falling asleep and rolling on top of the baby.

The Coroner then addressed the inquest jury, saying it was clear that the baby had died of suffocation. He commented that when being fed, the child was laid in the most dangerous position possible, and if the mother went to sleep she could easily have smothered it. The evidence of the position the child was put in was consistent with accidental death, but he spoke most strongly against mothers feeding children in this position, and believed it should be made against the law, as it was in other countries.

After considering the facts briefly, the jury returned a verdict of accidental death. Mrs Mould was returned to the asylum to continue her treatment. She was sent home in July, but after six weeks, she went back to the asylum. She was officially discharged as 'cured' on 14 December 1903.

On Boxing Day in 1903, the local newspapers reported that the Gloucester police were investigating a mysterious affair concerning one Mrs Agnes Mould, who had been detained by the police in connection with the disappearance of a little boy. Mrs Mould had recently been released from the County Lunatic Asylum at Wotton, where she had spent several months. She had gone missing during a shopping trip with her son, and when she was found some time later, she said that she had thrown a boy into the Gloucester and Berkeley Canal. Because of her previous mental health problems, her family had thought that she was having delusions, but when she persisted in her claim, she was taken to the police station. As no children had been reported missing, the police told her to go home. On Christmas Day, a family called Boulter who lived in Tudor Street, off Bristol Road, realised that their six-year-old-son, Hubert, was missing.

As a result, a search of the canal was carried out, and Mrs Mould was taken into custody.

The search for little Hubert Boulter continued through Christmas Day and Boxing Day, without success. The operation was resumed on Sunday, 27 December. Six dragnets were used, supplemented by the use of a large fishing net, loaned by Mr Walter Jelf. It was determined to sweep every foot of the canal for a considerable distance from the docks. This was impeded by the movement of steamers going up and down, but at about two o'clock in the afternoon, a police constable signalled that his dragnet had found something: this proved to be the body of Hubert Boulter. He was fully dressed, except his cap was missing. He was taken to the mortuary on the quay, where Mr Boulter identified the body of his son. The boy had been found at a spot between Two Mile Bend and the gas works, where Mr Boulter worked.

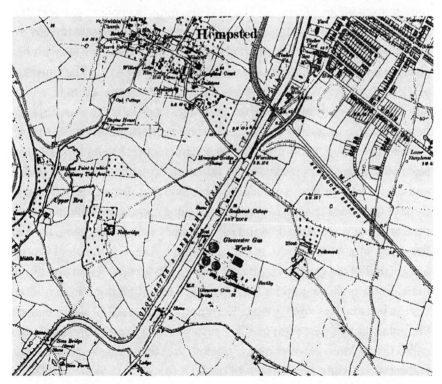

Detail from Ordnance Survey map of 1903, showing the Gloucester and Berkeley Canal. Two Mile Bend is bottom left. Tudor Street was one of those in the top right corner. (Author's collection)

On 28 December, an inquiry began at the Lower George Hotel – the same venue where the earlier inquest involving Agnes Mould had been held. The City Coroner, Charles Scott, led the inquiry into the circumstances of the death of six-year-old Hubert Thomas Boulter, the son of John and Emily Jane Boulter. Mr Scott outlined the case for the jury, and said Mrs Mould had been discharged from the asylum on 14 December. Two days later, she had been seen near Two Mile Bend and the bridge-keeper, thinking she was acting suspiciously, spoke to her and told her to go away.

On Christmas Eve, Mrs Mould and her son, who was about sixteen, had gone into the city to do some shopping when her son suddenly lost sight of her. A search was made by members of the family, and Mrs Mould's brother finally met her in Bristol Road and asked her what she had been doing. In reply, she said she had thrown a boy into the canal. He thought she was deluded, but she persisted in her statement. The next morning, the police were told that Hubert Boulter was missing. Mrs Mould had said that she saw the boy on a turning into Bristol Road, and had induced him to go for a walk with her down to the canal side, where she pushed him into the water. The daughter of the bridge-keeper saw the woman on the canal bank that evening, with a little boy. The girl's brother, who was walking along the bank some distance from the bridge, also saw a woman with a boy on the bank, and spoke to her.

Hubert's mother, Emily Jane Boulter, gave evidence. She had six children, and had last seen Hubert alive in the house on Christmas Eve, between five and six o'clock. She gave the children some food and afterwards Hubert and three of the others ran out to play. She put the youngest two children to bed, then at about seven o'clock in the evening she went out shopping, leaving her eldest son, who was ten, in charge of the house. Her husband was on a nightshift at the gas works. She got home at about ten o'clock and found her eldest son waiting up for her. She asked him if all the other children were in bed and he said they were. She went to bed herself at eleven o'clock. She got up at half past eight on Christmas morning to make breakfast, and called the children down at nine o'clock. It was then that she realised that Hubert was missing. She sent one of her boys to see if he was at Bristol Road police station, but he wasn't there.

In reply to a question from the jury foreman, Mrs Boulter said that she rarely went out and left her children. When asked why she hadn't checked that

Hubert was in bed when she got back from shopping, the distressed mother replied that she wouldn't have rested contented if she'd known the dear little fellow was not in. She loved her children too much for that. The Coroner then interposed, commenting that he thought there was no ground for the suggestion that Mrs Boulter did not look after her children properly. The police had made every inquiry and found her to be a thoroughly respectable woman.

Inspector Weaver said that on Christmas Day, having heard that the Boulter child was missing, he went to the Duke of Wellington and spoke to Mrs Mould. She cried and said she didn't know why she had done it. He arrested her later that evening and brought her in a cab to the city police station, where she was charged with murder.

He said that the place where the boy's body had been found was just above Two Mile Bend, about a mile and a half from the Boulters' house. On Christmas Day, the prints of a child's hobnailed boots were found on the canal bank, adjoining the towpath. They had been compared with the boy's boots, and the pattern of the nails was very similar. The prints were about 20 yards lower down from the spot where the body was found two days later. There was no flow of water in the canal, but assuming the boy went in at the point where the prints were found, his body might have been moved by the passage of the steamers going up and down. Other footprints were found on the bank in the same area, including one of a woman's boot. The prints of the boy's boots were in a slanting direction, while the woman's was straight with the canal. The bank was almost perpendicular there, and there would have been no chance of a child getting out.

Annie Priday lived with her parents at the Rea Bridge House, Quedgeley, about half a mile below Two Mile Bend. She said that on 24 December, at about half past six, she met a woman and a boy on the towpath. She and the woman looked each other full in the face. The friend that Annie was with remarked that the boy had no cap on. She and her friend went on to Gloucester. Returning home later, she told her mother what she had seen. It was a moonlit night, so she saw the woman's face clearly. She met the woman just above the old Pike House, a little above Two Mile Bend. She was sure the woman was the same one her father had spoken to on 16 December.

Arthur Thomas Priday, Annie's brother, also saw Mrs Mould and the boy on the towpath, at about ten minutes to seven. When he passed them, the steamship *Clio* was coming up the canal, and the light from the ship shone full on the woman's face. He said goodnight to her, but she didn't reply. He thought the boy looked quite comfortable.

William Moulder junior, aged sixteen, said he assisted his father in the bar of the Duke of Wellington. His mother had gone into Wotton Asylum in May. She stayed there for two months, then came home for six weeks, but then went back until 14 December. After coming home, she seemed fine at first, but the next day, at tea-time, she seemed unwell and wouldn't speak to anyone. About a week before Christmas, she went out for some time, and when she came back she wouldn't say where she had been. He noticed that she had muddy boots.

On Christmas Eve, at about half past two, he went shopping with his mother. They went into Bon Marché and bought toys for the children. While he was waiting for some change after paying, on looking round he found that his mother had disappeared. He searched up and down all the streets, but couldn't find her. He asked the police if they had seen her, and carried on looking, but finally went home, carrying the toys they had bought, and told his father, who was busy in the bar. Later, he went to his uncle, John Pollard, who eventually found Agnes and brought her home between nine

Old postcard of Northgate Street. Bon Marché is on the left-hand side of the street. (Author's collection)

and ten o'clock. Her boots were muddy. She sat in the same chair all night, with members of the family watching over her.

John Pollard, of 94 Alma Place, Bristol Road, was a stonemason and Mrs Mould's brother. He said that when his sister went missing for the first time, about a week before Christmas, he went to look for her and found her in Slaney Street at about half past eleven at night. She wouldn't say where she had been. On Christmas Eve, at about six o'clock in the evening, his nephew told him that his mother was missing again. He looked for her and eventually found her near the Avenue Hotel, on the corner of Bristol Road and Tuffley Avenue. She told him she had drowned a little boy. They walked together as far as Clifton Road. He asked her to show him where she had picked up the child, and she went back with him and pointed out a shop on the corner of Granville Street, saying she took him from there. She hadn't given him anything, but the little boy went with her willingly.

Pollard then brought her up Bristol Road again and asked her to come home, but she refused. He told her she must come home with him or go to the police station, and she said she would rather go to the latter than home. He started to get her in the direction of home, but going up Clifton Road, she said she was thirsty and pointed to a barber's shop as somewhere they could get a drink. When her brother told her they couldn't get a drink there, she refused to go any further. Finally, he took her to the police station in Bristol Road, where they saw Sergeant Hale. As no child had been reported missing, he was advised to take his sister home, which he did.

He went back to his own house briefly, then returned to the Duke of Wellington and stayed with his sister all night. He next saw her on Christmas Day, after dinner, when he thought that if anything she looked a little worse.

In reply to questions from the jury, he said he had never known her to behave strangely towards children before. He had no idea how she had got a child she didn't know to go off with her. Asked by the Coroner whether she had ever made peculiar statements about having done things, he replied only when she tried to do something to herself. She had told him one night that she had swallowed the ends off four boxes of matches – her husband had shown him the matches with all the tops off. Seventeen or eighteen

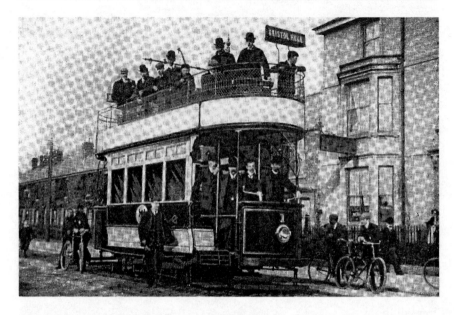

A tram in Bristol Road, 1904. (Author's collection)

years ago, she had swallowed a lot of pins and needles, but he didn't think she had suffered any ill effects. His sister was now thirty-eight, and had had six children.

In response to further questions, Pollard said he thought it would take about ten minutes to walk from the Avenue Hotel to Hempsted Bridge. He had gone to look for her down Bristol Road because the captain of a tug boat had told him she had been seen on the canal bank the week before.

In reply to a question from a juror, the Coroner said that Mrs Mould had been discharged from the asylum at the urgent request of herself and her husband. The hearing was then adjourned.

On the morning of Wednesday 30 December, a large number of people, chiefly women, went to the City Police Court, hoping to see the now infamous Agnes Mould. A crowd had also gathered at the back of Shire Hall, near the police station, where they expected Mrs Mould to be brought from the prison. They were to be disappointed, as it had been determined that Hubert Boulter's body had been found in the parish of Hempsted, outside the city boundary, meaning that the case was now under the jurisdiction of the county authorities.

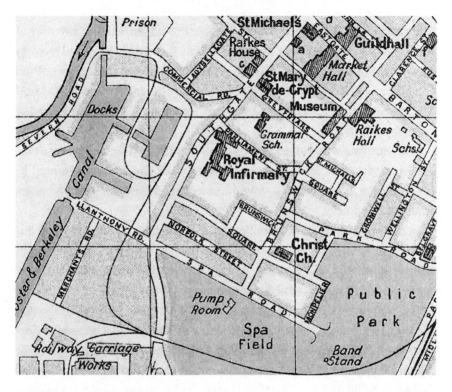

Detail from a 1924 map showing the Gloucester and Berkeley Canal. (Author's collection)

Mrs Mould appeared before a county magistrate at the police station on Wednesday afternoon. The proceedings, which lasted only a few minutes, took place in the office of the Deputy Chief Constable. Agnes was wearing a dark dress and a short blue jacket, a black-trimmed straw hat and had a black lace scarf around her neck. She had been quietly brought from the gaol to the police station, and was kept in the guard room under observation until she was taken before the magistrate. She had a care-worn, anxious expression, which made her look older than she really was. Inspector Weaver took her before the Chairman of the Gloucester County Bench, Revd C.E. Dighton. She sat with her head cast down, toying with a handkerchief, and appeared to take no notice of the proceedings. Deputy Chief Constable Harrison read out the charge, to which she made no answer. Agnes was charged with murder, and her case was adjourned until January.

On Saturday, 2 January 1904, another crowd gathered at the rear of Shire Hall, and again it was disappointed. As it was only intended to apply for a formal remand, Revd Dighton, DCC Harrison and Mr Bruce, from the office of the Magistrate's Clerk, went to the gaol to see Mrs Mould. She maintained her silence, and was further remanded until the following Saturday afternoon.

The inquest, which had been adjourned on 29 December, resumed on 4 January. Mrs Mould was not present but she was represented by Mr Armitage, who cross-examined some of the witnesses who had given evidence previously.

In reply to Mr Armitage, Mrs Boulter said she had never known her boy to stray away and play by the canal bank. He never went off alone at night, being a timid child, and was usually in the company of other children.

Inspector Weaver said he was present at the police station on 30 December, when Mrs Mould took part in an identity parade. She was placed in the hall of the station with five other women all dressed in dark clothing, about the same physical size, and three of them about the same age as Mrs Mould. When Annie Priday was brought in, she at once identified Mrs Mould, but her brother, Arthur Priday, at first could not identify the woman, and only did so after walking down the line slowly.

The Coroner asked Inspector Weaver about the whereabouts of the footprints which had been found on the canal bank. He replied that they were near Two Mile Bend, in the soft mud at the edge of the canal. The woman's footprint was about a foot away from the boy's. The body had been found twenty yards further down.

The Coroner then asked him if the statement made by Mrs Mould at the Duke of Wellington on Christmas morning was a voluntary one. The Inspector replied that it was. She was muttering to herself and crying, and he thought she seemed to know she had done something wrong. When he arrested her at about nine o'clock that evening, she appeared to be 'in great mental trouble'. She didn't speak to him at all after Christmas morning.

Finally, a new witness was called. William John Barnes, the husband of Mrs Mould's sister, Beatrice, said that on Christmas Day he had asked his sister-in-law how she was feeling, and she had replied, 'Oh, Bill, I have done something. I have drowned a little boy in the canal, and I shall get hung for it.' She repeated this several times and said she would not see Barnes again on this earth. Barnes hadn't believed her story, because she had said many things before for which there was no foundation.

The jury then considered the evidence, and returned a verdict that Hubert Boulter's death had been wilful murder, and the Coroner committed Mrs Mould to be tried at the next assizes.

On Tuesday, 5 January, the Governor of Gloucester Prison received a warrant issued by the Home Secretary, ordering that Agnes Mould should be removed from the prison to the County Asylum. She was taken there in the afternoon. The local press reported that it was expected that Mrs Mould would still appear before the County Magistrates on the coming Saturday, to face a charge of murder. However, on Thursday it was announced that she was to remain at the asylum for the time being.

In February, the Winter Assizes began in Gloucester and the name Agnes Dorcas Mould appeared on the Calendar of prisoners to be tried. The judge, Mr Justice Ridley, addressed the County Grand Jury concerning the cases they were to consider. He told them that the third case on the Calendar was that in which Agnes Dorcas Mould was charged with the wilful murder of Hubert Thomas Boulter, by pushing him into the Gloucester and Berkeley

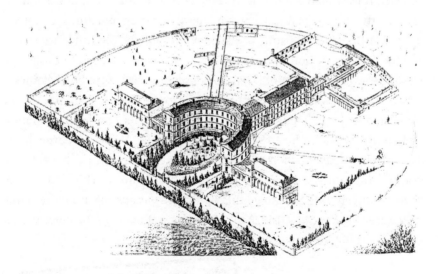

Isometric view of Gloucester Asylum by T. Fulljames, 1842.
(Gloucestershire Archives, D12733/1)

Canal. Under the name of the accused was written, 'Removed to the County Lunatic Asylum, 5th Jan 1904, by order of the Secretary of State.' The judge remarked that the woman was clearly a lunatic, and the Grand Jury would not be troubled by the matter, because of the Home Secretary's order. In other words, Agnes Mould was not to stand trial for her crime.

This was not, however, the end of the story. After Agnes Mould was returned to the asylum, now classified as a criminal lunatic, her husband was left to deal with some of the consequences of what she had done.

On 22 March 1904, a civil case was heard in the Gloucester County Court, before Judge Ellicott, in which John Boulter, of 1 Winifred Villas, Tudor Street, Gloucester, sued William Mould, publican of the Duke of Wellington and of High Street, Tredworth, for damages. Boulter was claiming £7 damages caused him as a consequence of the illegal act committed on 24 December 1903 by the wife of the defendant, in causing the death of Hubert Thomas Boulter, aged six years, son of the plaintiff, by pushing him into the canal at Gloucester.

The claim was made up of £2 funeral expenses and £5 other incidental expenses. When asked to give more details, the reply was that the burial and funeral expenses came to £2, while the other expenses were made up of: extra refreshments for bearers, etc., cost of a tailor to make a suit of black clothes for the plaintiff, black material and dress-making account for the plaintiff's wife, two suits of black clothes for the plaintiff's two sons, and the deceased's clothing, etc., spoilt, which was valued at ten shillings. The judge awarded the plaintiff ten shillings for the cost of the boy's clothes.

While Agnes Mould stayed in the Wotton Asylum, William Mould continued to live in Tredworth. As for the Boulter family, John and Emily had another child in late 1904, who they named Herbert George. John died in 1907, aged just forty-four. At the time of the 1911 census, Emily Boulter was living with all but her eldest child, and working as a laundress. Strangely, rather than getting as far away as possible from the canal, they were living at Sims Bridge in Quedgeley, not far from the place where little Hubert Boulter was drowned.

CASE SIX 1919

'I QUITE ADMIT I DID IT'

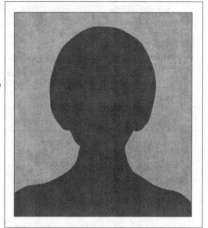

Suspect: Mildred Elizabeth Rodgers

Age: Thirty-two

Charge: Murder

Mildred Elizabeth Rodgers, known as Elizabeth, lived with her husband Matthew and their three sons in New Street, between Stroud Road and Park End Road. Elizabeth was the daughter of Eneas and Julia Ranford, and she had been born in Cheltenham in 1887, but her family had moved to Gloucester when she was an infant, and she and her brothers and sisters were brought up at 43 New Street. In 1908, Elizabeth married Matthew Rodgers, who was a few years her senior, at All Saints' Church, in Barton Street. The couple lived in various places, including Newcastle-under-Lyme in Staffordshire, which was Matthew's home town. By 1918, the Rodgers' had three sons, and the family moved back to Gloucester, into 45 New Street, next door to the house where Elizabeth was brought up. The occupants of no. 43 were Ernest and Maria Barnes, who had a thirteen-year-old son and a nine-month-old infant.

Mr and Mrs Rodgers' marriage was a tempestuous one and there were frequent quarrels, mostly concerning Matthew's relationships with other women. Matthew had joined the army in March 1915, and served with the 1/5th Lancashire Fusiliers. In 1918, he was injured and was placed in a Red Cross Hospital in Wilmslow, before being transferred to Manchester Infirmary. During that time, Elizabeth discovered that he had been courting a girl in Yorkshire, when she opened a letter which the young lady had innocently sent to his home address. Elizabeth went to see her husband in hospital to confront him, and for a while it seemed that the marriage was over, but she took him back.

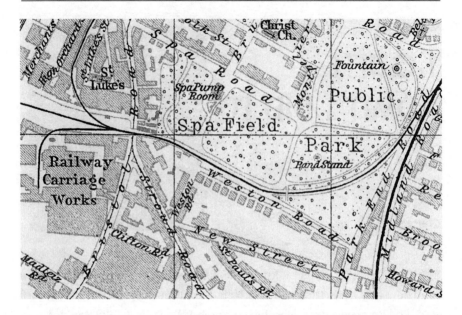

Detail from Baedeker's map of 1910, showing the New Street area. (Author's collection)

Matthew was discharged on 26 February 1919 and returned to the family home. The couple were soon having problems again, largely due to his relationship with a woman who lived in New Street, who was known locally as 'Hairy Mary'. Elizabeth frequently confided in her neighbour, Mrs Barnes, whom she had known for many years.

During the afternoon of Saturday, 13 September, the Barnes's heard an argument and a crashing sound in the kitchen next door. In the evening, Mr and Mrs Barnes went into the Park End Hotel, which was on the corner of New Street and Park End Road. They noticed Elizabeth Rodgers sitting at a table on her own, looking distressed. Mrs Barnes went and joined her, and Elizabeth asked her to have a drink with her, as it might be her last. She started to cry and, thinking she might be suicidal, Mrs Barnes told her not to be so silly and to think of the children.

At about half past ten, Matthew Rodgers came into the hotel. He went up to the counter and ordered a glass of beer. Elizabeth went over and spoke to him, then returned to her seat, while her husband went and joined his friends. Later, Matthew and Mr Barnes joined the women at their table, and the atmosphere seemed perfectly pleasant.

At eleven o'clock they all left the Park End Hotel and walked back to their houses. Matthew Rodgers then asked Mr and Mrs Barnes if they would like to come in and listen to some music. They agreed, and all went in to no. 45, where they were joined by the Barnes's son, who brought his infant brother with him. They all sat down to listen to the gramophone and Rodgers asked Mrs Barnes if he could hold the baby, then he sat in his chair with the little boy on his knee. As well as listening to the gramophone, Mr Barnes played a melodeon, and there was also some singing.

At about half past midnight, Elizabeth Rodgers suddenly got up from her seat by the fire and went into the back room. She returned a few minutes later, went up behind her husband's chair and put her arms around his neck, as if she was going to kiss him. Then she drew away quickly and left the room. Matthew Rodgers immediately slumped forward and the baby fell off his knee, but landed safely on the sofa where Mr Barnes was sitting. The horrified guests realised that a stream of blood was gushing from Rodgers' neck.

Mrs Barnes picked up her baby and ran from the house; Mr Barnes carried the injured man out on to the pavement, and someone went to get

'a stream of blood was gushing from Rodgers' neck'

the police. Elizabeth Rodgers waited calmly on her doorstep for the police to arrive and take her into custody. Matthew Rodgers was taken to the infirmary, but he was already dead.

The trial of Mildred Elizabeth Rodgers began on 28 October 1919, before Mr Justice Rowlatt. The public gallery in the courtroom was full as the prisoner, neatly dressed in black, was brought into the dock, accompanied by two female prison warders. In reply to the charge that she had wilfully and with malice aforethought murdered her husband, she pleaded not guilty in a clear and distinct voice.

Mr Cockburn opened the case for the prosecution. He told the jury that the unhappy woman sitting in the dock was accused of the awful crime of murdering her husband and respectfully asked that if any of them had heard or read in the newspapers about the case, or had spoken with their friends about it, that they now banish from their minds any impressions they might have formed. In common fairness to the prisoner, and in the general cause of justice, it was essential that the jury should approach the case with free and open minds.

The prisoner worked as a factory hand, and her husband was a boot-repairer by trade. For about the last eighteen months the Rodgers family had lived at 45 New Street. For some time there had been serious quarrels between husband and wife, chiefly in respect of the

A page from the *Cheltenham Chronicle and Gloucestershire Graphic* for 20 September 1919, showing 45 New Street, the Barnes's son and baby, Mr Barnes, the Rodgers' children, and Mrs Barnes. (Gloucestershire Archives)

The courthouse, behind Shire Hall. (Jill Evans)

deceased man's relationships with other women. The jury would hear particular mention of one woman, a Mrs Smith, who would be referred to in the case by her nickname of 'Hairy Mary', and who also lived in New Street.

The two principal witnesses for the Crown would be Mr and Mrs Ernest Charles Barnes, who lived next door to the prisoner and her husband, at 43 New Street. The jury would hear from the Barnes's that on 13 September a somewhat violent quarrel between the prisoner and her husband was heard, and it was on the evening of the same day, and on into the night, that occurred the events which led to the death of Mr Rodgers. It was, Mr Cockburn said, a tragedy in two scenes. The first scene took place in the Park End Hotel and the second scene was in the home of the prisoner and the deceased.

Florence Maria Barnes, wife of Ernest Barnes, was the first witness called. She had known Elizabeth Rodgers for twenty years and had lived next door to her for the past eighteen months. She had often heard quarrels next door, and Mrs Rodgers had complained to her about her husband carrying on with other women. Mrs Barnes then related what had happened at the Park End Hotel, and subsequently at 45 New Street.

Cross-examined by Mr Lort-Williams, the defence counsel, she said Mrs Rodgers had always been a woman of good character and an excellent mother, looking after her children as well as she could. Whilst her husband was away at war, Mrs Rodgers had worked hard to keep things

The Park End Hotel, on the corner of New Street and Park End Road. (Jill Evans)

together and had made a comfortable little home. She had constantly made complaints about her husband's behaviour, and about him going about with other women and threatening to go about with them as much as he wanted. She had shown Mrs Barnes two letters sent to her by her husband. These letters were then produced in court and read out to the jury. The first one read:

Just a few lines in answer to your insult offered when you sent me the photo. I may as well tell you the best thing you can do is to try and take proceedings for a divorce as soon as you can, as my affection for you is dead, and I have found someone I like better, and you can take proceedings to get me divorced. The last two letters I had from you poisoned my heart against you forever. You can have who you like, as I have found someone to care for me better than you. So I set you free to do as you like, as I am willing to keep my children, but as for you I have finished for ever. I still remain a rotter and fool in your eyes, but a man in someone else's who I can trust and who knows how to respect a man in return. I send my best and fondest love to my children, Matt, George and Jack. From their ever loving Father, M. Rodgers.

You can start as soon as you like, and I will give you all the proof you like; so carry on as soon as you can as I want to be free from you.

The second letter read:

My dear wife and children. Just a few lines in answer to your letter. I am very sorry if I hurt your feelings in any way, as I did not mean anything by what I put in my letter to you, and I am very sorry for writing such a foolish letter. As I have been in front of my commanding officer, and he made me look like a big fool, and I was very lucky I did not get into trouble for it, but he gave me a good talking to and told me to write to you and apologise for the letter I wrote to you. I hope you will forgive me for writing such a foolish letter; so give my best love to Matty, George and Jackie, and xxx for yourself. I remain your ever-loving husband. xxxx for you and the children.

Dear Bess,- All I can see is that we are both jealous of one another, and it is that which is the cause of all the trouble, but I can tell you it will never occur again so just write me a nice letter and say you will forgive me, and I will act as a man should do in the future. Dear Bess, love and xxxx to you and the children. From Matt to Bess, with love and xxxx.

Mrs Barnes said Mrs Rodgers told her she had forgiven her husband, but later on she made complaints about him and other women. Mr Rodgers had no cause to be jealous concerning his wife, for she had never heard or known of her carrying on with any other man. Since Matthew Rodgers had returned from the army, his wife had continued to work and keep the children, but Mrs Barnes had never known him to do a day's work since he came home.

The photograph referred to by Matthew Rodgers in his first letter was one of a woman which had been sent to the Rodgers' eldest son, Matt, upon which were the words, 'This will soon be your new Mammy.' Mrs Barnes knew 'Hairy Mary', and Matthew Rodgers had lived with her before he married the prisoner.

At the Park End Hotel on Saturday night, Mrs Rodgers told Mrs Barnes that her husband had 'come home nasty' in the afternoon, and had smashed some crockery and finished up by throwing some dirty water over the kitchen. Mrs Rodgers told her that he had pawned a watch she had given him as a present to get money to treat 'Hairy Mary'. She asked her to come to her assistance if her husband 'knocked her about' that night. Mrs Barnes told her she ought never to have had him back. Mrs Rodgers was in a state, crying one minute and laughing the next.

Police Constable Pinnions deposed that he went to New Street on the night in question and saw the body of Rodgers lying on the pavement and the prisoner standing at the door. PC Hendry stated that in the course of searching the house, he found a bloodstained razor on a window ledge in the yard. Police Sergeant Glover said he arrived at New Street with the two constables and saw Mrs Rodgers standing at her door. He cautioned her and she said, 'Yes, this is my husband. He has been carrying on with another woman.

I quite admit I did it.' She handed the Sergeant three letters and said, 'These will show you what he has been doing.'

These letters were then read out in court. The first was headed, 'Private M. Rodgers, 1/5 Lancashire Fusiliers, Red Cross Hospital, Wilmslow, Cheshire, September 28, 1918'. It referred to the young lady in Yorkshire, whose letter had caused Elizabeth to go to the hospital to confront her husband. It read:

Dear Bess,

Just a few lines to you. Hope you got back safe, and that you found the children quite safe. I was sorry I could not come back to the station to see you off, but I was so cut up with seeing you it was only agony for me to try and speak to you, but you can have a contented mind that I have made up my mind to finish it off altogether with that girl, and the reason why I did not give you the address is I know what kind of letter you would have sent to her. So you can tell Matt, George and Jack not to upset themselves about me, as I have made my mind up to be the same as I used to be, and to turn over a new leaf. So I hope you will try to forget it all and destroy them letters I sent you, and I will write you a long letter next time, as I don't hardly know how to write to you.

Dear Bess, the doctor came and seen all in the hospital, and he marked some of them out, but he did not say anything to me, but I think if he had examined me he would have said I had heart failure, as you gave me the biggest shock I ever had in my life, and I can tell you I have not got over it yet. So give my best love and kisses to Matt, George and Jack, and the same to you when you have cooled down a bit.

From your ever-loving husband and father, Matt Rodgers.

To this letter were added a number of kisses with 'for the children from Daddie', then followed a lot more kisses and 'You can have these, if you will accept them.'

The next letter showed that Mrs Rodgers had found out the address of the girl who was the subject of the above. Miss Crabtree wrote from Yorkshire:

Dear Mrs Rodgers,

I have received your letter, and when I opened it what a shock I got – I could not open my lips for a few minutes. I handed the letter to my mother, and she read it aloud and when she had finished she says 'What do you think of him now?' Because he always swore to me that he was a single young man, and if there is anything I hate its married men or women to go about with single men or women. I think they can find something else to do, and what is more I think you have misjudged me. If I had known he had been married I would never have written a line to him, but I would have told him he ought to be ashamed of himself and he ought to look after his wife and children before looking to other girls.

I never thought there were such people in the world. I shall never trust anyone. I have never gone about with boys much, because I am home too much to go about with anyone. But my father is raging mad over it. If he had been near him when the letter came I don't know what he would have done to him. I am sure my family are all respectable and as for disgracing them I would rather die than disgrace them – I think too much about my home and people.

Mother says you should get to know a person before you judge them. I can just imagine how hard it would be for you. It must have been awful when you opened the letter. You have no idea how sorry we all are and for the children, but I never wish to see him or hear from him again. I shall never trust another man as long as I live. I think men are all alike – they are best left alone. And I am glad you have let me know so soon, but I am thankful everything is as it is. I have not done anything to be ashamed, only I would not like to think I had upset anyone's home, because I am sure I would not do it and know about it. I can tell you if I have put any-thing in this letter you don't believe, you can always come and see for yourself. Then you can see with looking what we are without asking. Now I will close.

Miss Crabtree.

The third letter was from Matthew Rodgers, who was now in a ward at Manchester Infirmary:

My dear Wife and Children, - Just a few lines in answer to your letter and I am pleased to hear that the children are still keeping in the best of health, as it leaves me the same at present. I have had enough of this sort of letter-writing, and I want a proper answer from you as to what you intend doing, as I am not going to keep wasting money on stamps. So just write and let me know if you are willing to make things up again or not, and if you don't intend to try to be the same as we were before, just let me know and I will know what to do, as I don't think I will be in hospital much longer, and I want to know what you intend to do, for if you have been telling all the street about what I have done, well it will be as well for me to keep away and allow you so much a week after your money is stopped, as you will not be getting it much longer now, so you want to be prepared, for as soon as I am discharged from the Army your pay will stop, so I want a proper answer from you.

Give my best love to Mattie, George and Jack, and take some for yourself, if I am not too low to be thought about. I remain your Husband and Father, Matt. R.

Old postcard of Manchester Infirmary. (Author's collection)

To this letter were added kisses 'for the children' and the words, 'Waiting for your reply and my letters you have.'

Sergeant Glover continued his evidence, saying he took Mrs Rodgers to the police station and on the way there she was attacked by the woman Smith ('Hairy Mary'). At the police station, she admitted that she had killed her husband, adding, 'He said my children were all bastards and that he could go with Hairy Mary when he liked.' As Gloucester Prison was an all-male institution, the Sergeant took Mrs Rodgers to Horfield Prison in Bristol. On the way there, she said to him,

> When I was in the Park End Hotel my husband came to me and showed me an apple and said, 'Do you see this apple? It is what my fancy girl gave to me.' I told him to put it back in his pocket, as it was no credit to him to show me up in front of people. Mrs Rowles heard him say it, and saw him with the apple. He put it back in his pocket.

Glover confirmed that an apple was found in the pocket of one of the deceased man's coats.

Inspector Brotheridge said that the prisoner was left in his charge for a few minutes at the police station. She told him,

> He has always treated me badly ever since we were married, and I have always worked hard and kept respectable. He bets on horses. Tonight he was nursing another woman's baby and wanted to buy it for a sovereign, and said to me that all my three children were bastards. That did it. I could stand it no more. Look after my three children, Inspector, won't you.

The House Surgeon at the Gloucestershire Royal Infirmary stated that when Rodgers was brought in, he was already dead. The whole of his neck had been severed, except for the spinal column.

Mr Lort-Williams then began his address to the jury on behalf of the prisoner. He stated that the jury had three verdicts to consider: guilty of murder; guilty of manslaughter under great provocation; or not guilty of any crime. Although he did not suggest that the prisoner was not guilty of any crime, he did ask the jury,

... how could this unfortunate woman against whom no one could say a single word have come to the position of committing a murder? Was not she gradually worked up to such a pitch of mental agony week by week, day by day, culminating on September 13th in a series of acts of mental cruelty? Was not she worked up to such a pitch upon that night that it only required one further small act to make her provoked to such an extent that she could not command the ordinary moral ideas which should have forbidden her to commit such a crime? If so, the jury would have a duty to say that the woman was guilty not of murder but of manslaughter – the killing of a human being upon very great provocation.

The accused had borne an excellent character as a hard-working woman and a good mother. They all sympathised with the poor creature whose life had been taken; for whatever his misdeeds, death was too great a penalty for him to have paid. It had been shown that Rodgers was a bad husband and, except for a show of affection to his children, he was not a good father either. He was constantly going about with other women and neglecting his home, and he made his conduct infinitely worse by writing to his wife about his episodes with other women. At least he might have had the decency to keep those particulars to himself. It was difficult to come to the conclusion that Mrs Rodgers had the mind of a murderess and Mr Lort-Williams suggested that the jury should find her guilty of manslaughter.

The judge began his summing up by explaining to the jury that murder was

The Rodgers' boys, aged eleven, five and seven. Detail from the *Cheltenham Chronicle and Gloucestershire Graphic*, 20 September 1919. (Gloucestershire Archives)

killing a person on purpose without excuse, but it might be reduced to manslaughter by great provocation. The doctrine of provocation was not a concession to vindictiveness, but to the impulses of human temper. In this case, the bad conduct of the victim was not provocation in law, but those acts of the deceased might have had the result of reducing the prisoner to a state of mind which meant she needed very little further provocation than would otherwise have been the case. The question was, what provocation, if any, took place immediately before the blow was struck?

Nobody disputed that Elizabeth had killed her husband. She took a razor and applied it to his throat with such determination that, but for the backbone, his head would have been cut off. A great appeal had been made to the jury on behalf of the prisoner, but the jury had a duty to perform which must be done dispassionately.

As to what happened just before the tragedy, the judge was not satisfied that the jury had heard the whole story: he dared say that the memories

Mrs Rodgers, in the *Cheltenham Chronicle and Gloucestershire Graphic*, 20 September 1919. (Gloucestershire Archives)

of Mr and Mrs Barnes were a little impaired by the shock of what had happened. It was difficult to believe that they had heard the whole story of what happened immediately before the woman went out and fetched the razor. It was an astonishing thing that with nothing happening – merely the deceased dangling the baby on his knees – the prisoner would have suddenly got up, fetched the razor and committed the crime. The judge thought it was possible that Rodgers, going on remarks made by him to his wife in the past, said something intolerable to her. There must have been something said or done which made the prisoner go out and get the razor. He was bound to say that everything pointed to this being an absolutely sudden act, and the court was without any knowledge at all of what it was that precipitated the crisis at that moment.

The judge finished by saying that in this case he thought that if the jury could only explain the sudden action of Mrs Rodgers by assuming that something was done by speech or gesture by the deceased which was intolerable to Elizabeth, and that she in a moment of passion and without deliberation cut his throat, then the jury would be entitled to return a verdict of manslaughter.

The jury then retired, and after an absence of about six minutes returned to court with a verdict of guilty of manslaughter under great provocation. Elizabeth Rodgers was then brought up to be sentenced, supported on either side by a female warder. Mr Lort-Williams made an appeal for mercy, adding that the prisoner believed she was pregnant. The judge, in passing sentence, said the jury had taken a very merciful view of the case, which they were only able to take by assuming certain possibilities, in support of which there was no evidence. He could not help thinking that it was a case very near to murder. He was extremely sorry for the prisoner, but he could not treat her with great leniency because she killed her husband with the greatest possible determination. He was sorry to say he must sentence her to penal servitude, but only for five years.

Elizabeth Rodgers said nothing in response, and was taken down to the cells.

'I DON'T KNOW WHERE I HIT HIM. I LOST MY HEAD'

Suspect:	Ronald Wells
Age:	Nineteen
Charge:	Murder

On the west side of Gloucester Cathedral there is an archway known as St Mary's Gate, which leads into an area called St Mary's Square. Houses and buildings surround the ancient church of St Mary de Lode, and between the church and the gate there stands a monument to Bishop Hooper, who was burnt at the stake on that spot in 1555. Most of the houses which once enclosed the church and monument have long since been demolished, and modern buildings have taken their place.

In 1934, George Wells was the occupant of 48 St Mary's Square, which was on the corner with Mount Street. He was a larger-than-life man, both in build and character, and was well known in Gloucester and the surrounding villages. Born in Kent, in his youth he had travelled the world, getting work where he could. In 1914, Wells married Matilda Silvester in Taunton, Somerset, and they had two children, Frances Mary and Ronald George. The family moved to Gloucester when Ronald was a baby, but his mother left when he was six years old. Ronald stayed with his father while Frances, who was then eight, went to live with a family in nearby Corse.

George Wells worked for many years as a slaughter man, and was employed for a long time by Messrs Smith Bros, butchers, who had a shop in Westgate Street. Later, he started up a business as a cheese-hawker and used to travel around in a pony and trap, selling his wares. In May 1934,

Sketch of St Mary's Square in *The Century* magazine, 1890. (Author's collection)

Wells was involved in an accident, in which a motorcycle collided with his pony and trap. He was thrown from the trap and his collarbone was broken. He had a weakness in his right arm after that, and was due to be paid some compensation money as a result of the accident.

Ronald Wells attended Archdeacon Street School until he was fourteen, then worked at Messrs Smith Bros shop, and helped his father in the slaughterhouse for about nine months. Afterwards, he found employment at various shops, but in October 1930 he was brought before the Gloucester Juvenile Court, charged with attempting to break into a shop where he had previously worked. He was bound over for two years and put on probation. In 1932, when he was seventeen, he was tried at the assizes on charges of shop-breaking, larceny and breach of recognizances, and was sentenced to three years in a borstal.

In July 1934, Ronald Wells was released on licence and went back to live with his father at 48 St Mary's Square. He also joined his father in the cheese-selling business. Father and son appeared to get on well together, although there were sometimes arguments about Ronald staying out late at night, drinking. George Wells had put his son in charge of looking after the money from the business, but soon had to bring someone in to show Ronald how to keep accounts properly.

George Wells in *The Citizen*, 30 January 1935. (Gloucestershire Archives)

Towards the end of October 1934, neighbours realised that George Wells had not been seen for some time, although Ronald was observed going in and out of the house. Frederick Williams lived at 2 Mount Street, and his house adjoined 48 St Mary's Square. George Wells had a bad chest, which meant he would cough frequently. Williams could hear this clearly through his wall, but the last time he noticed the coughing was in the early hours of 21 October. He also heard Wells tell his son that if he continued to stay out late, he would have to find somewhere else to live. A couple of days later, not having heard Wells at all, he asked Ronald where his father was, and he replied that he was lying low for a couple of days, 'on account of that compensation job'. Williams took this to mean it had something to do with the money Wells was due to receive from his accident. When Williams mentioned that he hadn't heard Wells coughing for a while, Ronald said that the cough had gone.

Gilbert Aitcheson, who was friends with both father and son, saw the two of them riding in their pony and trap on the afternoon of 22 October. The following day, Ronald asked Aitcheson to go out with him in the trap. When Aitcheson inquired where his father was, the lad replied that he was ill and was not getting up today. While they were out, they had a slight accident and Aitcheson hurt his knee. Later that day, Ronald went to see him and said his father wanted to know if his knee hurt much. Aitcheson said he would come over in a few minutes to speak to him. Ronald left, but

Old postcard of St Mary's Square. (Author's collection)

returned shortly after to tell him his father had gone to bed. After that, Aitcheson frequently asked after George Wells, and Ronald would usually reply that he was 'no better, no worse'. On 30 October, Aitcheson went to a party with Ronald. They met outside no. 48 and, before closing the door, Ronald called upstairs, 'Goodnight Dad, I shan't be long.'

On 31 October, Ronald's sister, Frances, arrived at the door and asked how her father was. Ronald replied that he had been ill in bed with bronchitis, but he was now out, 'up the street'. She did not enter the house.

When November arrived and there was still no sign of George Wells, Aitcheson asked Ronald if his father was 'doing time'. Ronald then said that his father was in prison in Cheltenham for a month, because he hadn't paid a fine for a minor offence, and they had been trying to keep it quiet. Aitcheson told him that the neighbours were talking about breaking into the house, and Ronald told him to say his father was in Cheltenham hospital. Aitcheson noticed that Ronald had his blue suit on, rather than his working clothes, and asked him why. He replied that he was going to see his father. Aitcheson saw Ronald go off on his bicycle later that day, and when the young man had not come back by the next day, Aitcheson called the police.

At twenty past two on the afternoon of 2 November, Inspector Large and Detective Sergeant Ward arrived at 48 St Mary's Square and gained entry to the house through a window. All the doors in the living room were closed. Ward opened the door that closed off the stairs and saw the body of George Wells lying halfway up, on the landing, with its back against the wall and the legs hanging down the stairs. The body was covered with an overcoat and the head had a piece of a vest placed over it. His face, head and hands were covered in blood, but he was wearing a clean shirt. Next to the body was a case of butcher's knives, which were clean and had not been used.

There was no sign of blood upstairs in the bedroom, but bloodstains were found downstairs in the living room, on the ceiling, pictures, crockery on the dresser and wallpaper. The floor of the living room, unlike the rest of the house, was extremely clean. There was a couch in front of the

'a bundle of blood-stained clothes'

fireplace with some blankets on it, as if someone had been using it as a makeshift bed.

There were some marks of blood on the door of the scullery, and inside the police found a bundle of bloodstained clothes, including the other part of the vest which had been placed over the dead man's head. Two shirts were hanging on a line in the scullery, apparently belonging to Ronald from their size. Both had bloodstains on them. In the coal cellar, a heavy hammer with a sharp end was found, on which were traces of blood.

That evening, a police appeal was broadcast by the BBC, asking listeners to look out for Ronald George Wells, who was wanted in connection with the death of his father, George Wells. He was described as being five feet six inches in height, of medium build, with fair hair and blue eyes, clean shaven but with a prominent cut on his right lip, a large nose which inclined to the right, and he stammered when speaking. He had last been seen at about twenty past two on 1 November, in Gloucester, riding a man's old bicycle.

The following evening, Ronald Wells walked into the police station at Woolaston, in the Forest of Dean, and asked for something to eat. He had no money and appeared exhausted. The police constable on duty recognised him from his description and sent a message to Gloucester. Wells was taken to the central police station in Gloucester, where he was charged by Deputy Chief Constable Hopkins with murder. He denied the charge.

Ronald George Wells in *The Citizen*, 29 January 1935. (Gloucestershire Archives)

On 5 November, Ronald Wells appeared before a magistrate at Gloucester police station. A crowd of about 100 people waited outside, hoping to see the youth, but he was already in the cells of the building. The hearing was held in the clerk's office at the police station, before the mayor and other magistrates. Wells seemed calm and stood rigidly to attention throughout the hearing. Deputy Chief Constable Hopkins related how the body had been found on 2 November. Wells was remanded for eight days.

On the same day, an inquest into the death of George Wells was opened by the City Coroner, Trevor Wellington. At this time it was only intended to formally identify the deceased man, so a burial order could be issued. Frederick Williams identified the body and then the inquest was adjourned.

On 7 November, George Wells, who was about sixty-two years old, was buried at Gloucester cemetery. It was a bitterly cold day with a strong northerly wind, yet hundreds of onlookers gathered to watch the hearse arrive. The coffin was covered with wreaths from friends and neighbours, and a dozen mourners followed the hearse in two motor coaches. The local newspapers revealed that Wells had left no money or estate with which to pay for a funeral, and the authorities would have buried him in a pauper's grave but for his former employers, Messrs Smith Bros, who had come forward with an offer to pay for his burial.

Ronald Wells appeared in court and was remanded twice more before his case was finally heard on 27 November. His mother, who he hadn't seen since he was six, was in the court, and smiled at her son as he sat down.

It was revealed that George Wells had seven or eight wounds to his head and neck, and a puncture wound over his right eye which had penetrated the brain. The injuries had been inflicted by a blunt instrument with a pointed end. The doctor who carried out the post-mortem, William Washbourn, believed Wells had been struck while sitting down in his chair. The doctor summised that Wells had died sometime between 18 and 24 October, but from the evidence of the neighbours, probably on 22 or 23 October.

At the end of the hearing, Ronald George Wells was committed for trial at the assizes.

The trial began at Gloucester on 29 January 1935, before Mr Justice Hawke. A crowd had gathered outside,

Justice Hawke and the County High Sheriff in *The Citizen*, 3 February 1940. (Gloucestershire Archives)

hoping to gain admission, but many were left disappointed as the court-room quickly filled up. While waiting for the trial to start, Ronald Wells had been held in Gloucester Prison. He was brought to the court early in the morning, when the streets were still deserted. When he was led into the dock between two warders he looked slightly flushed, but was other-wise calm. He wore the same navy blue suit in which he had been arrested. His mother took a seat directly behind the dock.

The case for the prosecution was led by Mr St John Micklethwait KC, while Mr Cotes-Preedy KC defended the prisoner. The jury consisted of nine men and three women. Silence fell in the court as Judge Hawke took his seat and the Clerk read out the charge, to which Wells replied in a firm voice, 'Not guilty.'

Mr Micklethwait then began to outline the case for the prosecution, telling the jury that the story he had to tell was 'a gruesome and horrible one'. He described how the police had entered the house in St Mary's

Front page of *The Citizen*, 29 January 1935. (Gloucestershire Archives)

Square on 2 November and found George Wells lying dead on the stairs. The case for the prosecution was that Wells had been killed downstairs in the sitting room, where all the bloodstains were found. His shirt and vest were removed and a clean shirt put on his body, which was then carried upstairs as far as the landing. The head and torso were then covered and the body left there for a number of days.

Mr Micklethwait told the jury that the defence counsel would suggest that Ronald had killed his father in self-defence, because the older man, who was bigger and stronger, had attacked him. However, the neighbours, who could hear coughing and sometimes conversations through the walls, had not been aware of any disturbance, fight or quarrel. Moreover, the prosecution would argue that Mr Wells had been struck from behind while he was sitting in a chair.

The case for the defence largely concentrated on the idea that George Wells was a man with a violent temper. Detective Sergeant Ward, after giving his evidence about finding Wells's body, was asked by Mr Cotes-Preedy if he had discovered in the course of his enquiries that Wells was a violent man. Ward replied that the neighbours had said Wells was a very hot-tempered man. He wouldn't like to say that he had been violent – more hasty tempered. Ward also said in reply to a question from Mr Cotes-Preedy that he understood that at the age of nine, Ronald Wells was made to work with his father at slaughtering.

Frederick Williams said he had been living at 2 Mount Street when Mrs Wells was still with her husband. He believed they parted because Wells used to come home sometimes and start 'carrying on'. Asked if Wells was brutal to her, Williams replied that she ran out of the house on several occasions and stayed away for some time. He believed she had been frightened of her husband. Regarding Wells's temper, Williams recalled how on one occasion Wells had gone for him with a whip in his hand, but, 'I stood up to him and served him in the same way'. He said that Ronald Wells had been staying out late, which had annoyed his father.

Detective Constable Franklin said he had known George Wells for about eleven years. Asked by Mr Cotes-Preedy whether Wells was a man with a violent temper, he said, 'I would not describe him as strongly as that. I would say he had a very hasty temper.'

Dr William Washbourn, the police surgeon who had conducted the post-mortem on the body, said George Wells was five feet ten inches tall, muscular and well-developed. Death took place some time between a week and a fortnight before his examination of the body. Wells's death had been due to extensive fracture of the skull, resulting in concussion and shock. All the blows had been given by the hammer found, some with the sharp end and some with the flat end, and he believed they had been inflicted from behind.

Mr Cotes-Preedy said, 'I presume it is only surmise on your part when you tell the jury that you think the blows may have been struck while the father was sitting down?' Dr Washbourn agreed that it was. It was possible that most of the wounds could have been applied from the front, but not the one at the back of the head. Dr Washbourne conceded that the wound at the back of the head might possibly have been caused if Wells's head had fallen forward after being struck a few times before.

Mr Cotes-Preedy then called to the witness box Dr Graham, the medical officer of Gloucester Prison, who had assessed the mental state of Ronald

Wells and sent a report to the Director of Public Prosecutions. He said that Wells was a highly strung, nervy and temperamental youth, who, when faced with a sudden emergency, would be likely to overreact.

At half past five, a hush fell in the courtroom as Ronald Wells entered the witness box. He seemed calm, but owing to his pronounced stammer, his voice could not be heard in the court. His words were repeated for the judge and jury by Mr Musson, the defence counsel who examined him.

Wells said that on 22 October 1934 he got home at about a quarter to eleven. His father had sat up waiting for him and was angry. He sat down on a chair in the living room to take off his boots. His father went to get some coal for the fire and came back holding the coal hammer. Wells heard him say, 'I'll teach you to come here like this. You won't go out of here again.'

Realising that his father had raised the hammer, Ronald jumped up and pushed him towards his armchair, then grappled with him for the weapon. He managed to wrench it away but then his father came at him to get it back. He realised he would have to hit him to stop him getting the hammer again. So he hit his father, and lost his head, and continued hitting him. The next thing he knew, his father was on the ground. He lifted him into his armchair, which was a struggle, but he managed it. Then he sat down in his chair and looked at his father. Later, he went out to the scullery to wash his hands and face, which had blood on them. He went back into the living room and put some coal on the fire, and then sat in his chair all night.

At about five the next morning he woke from a doze and saw that his father was dead. He lifted him out of the chair, because he was afraid someone might come in. There was blood all over his father's smock and shirt, so he laid him on the ground and took them off, and put a clean shirt on him. He wanted to take him upstairs and lay him on the bed, but he couldn't get the body round the corner on the landing, so he had to leave him there, halfway up the stairs.

He didn't tell anyone what had happened because he was afraid. He had no one to confide in and wanted time to think it out. He went halfway to the police station several times, but was too afraid to carry on. He slept for several nights on the couch, in front of the fire. He scrubbed the floor because there was blood all over it. The hammer was under the table all night, then he put it in the coal cellar.

On 1 November, he took some clothes to Mrs Taylor's shop to sell, because he had no money. He went to Hereford with the money he got from that, then went about selling cheese. After Hereford, he went to Abergavenny, Pontypool and Cardiff, all on the same day. Then he went to Newport and spent a night in a lodging house there. He couldn't pay his bill, so left his bicycle and his father's watch. He then walked as far as Woolaston, where he handed himself in at the police station.

Having given the main part of his evidence, the judge adjourned the trial until the following morning. The members of the jury were put up overnight in the Ram Hotel, in Southgate Street.

On the following morning, Ronald Wells was cross-examined by Mr Micklethwait. In reply to questioning, Wells said he began to help his father in the cheese-hawking business in July. His father put him in charge of the money and he had got someone to show him how to keep accounts properly, but he denied that his father had complained there was not so much money coming in from the business as there ought to have been, or that there was trouble between him and his father over money matters.

Wells admitted that he had begun to stay out late, going to public houses, and this had caused quarrels. Asked where he got the money to go to public houses, Wells replied that he could take what he wanted.

Old postcard of Southgate Street, with the Ram Hotel on the left. (Author's collection)

He denied that he gambled with money he received from selling cheese, or that he went to greyhound races. His father usually went to bed at about half past nine, and on the night of 22 October he had come home at about a quarter to eleven. His father was sitting up in his chair and started grumbling about him being out so late: 'He shouted at me and asked where I had been.'

Asked why his father had gone to get coal for the fire at that time of night, Wells replied that he did not know, adding, 'I thought it was unusual.' He also didn't know why his father would have brought the coal hammer back with him. Asked why he did not escape through the scullery, Wells replied that it would have been impossible from where he was, without the risk of being hit. Asked about the blows he inflicted on his father, Wells replied, 'I don't know where I hit him. I lost my head.' He wasn't angry when he hit his father, just afraid. He had been sorry for what he had done. Asked why he didn't get a doctor, he said he knew it was too late to save him. He hadn't placed the case of knives on the stairs – they were always kept there.

Wells admitted that he had gone to public houses occasionally after that night. In fact, he had been to the Leather Bottle in Archdeacon Street nearly every night. He had also gone to a party in the Forest of Dean. Pressed to say why he hadn't told the neighbours what had happened, Wells said he had wanted time to think. Asked why he had not told the truth when he was arrested, he said they didn't ask him to explain, just arrested him, and he told them he didn't murder his father. Mr Micklethwait said, 'I suggest to you that this story is quite untrue, that your father was sitting in the arm-chair, and that you got the hammer and hit him while he was sitting down.'

'I didn't,' Wells replied, in a low voice.

Mr Mickelthwait then began his final address to the jury, and said that to reduce a charge of murder to one of manslaughter he had to prove that the act of killing someone was justified, because it had been done in self-defence. He could hardly imagine that the rain of blows they had heard about on this occasion had been justified. If Wells's story of his father attacking him was true, then after getting the hammer off him, all he had to do was run away. It was quite clear that there had been rows between father and son over the latter's staying out late drinking. However, the only threat the father had made to his son was that he would have to find new lodgings. Was it not instead true, as Dr Washbourn suggested, that George Wells was struck from behind when he was sitting in his chair? Ronald Wells had said there had been a struggle with his father, but the neighbours hadn't heard a thing, although they usually knew if George even coughed.

In his address, Mr Cotes-Preedy said he was going to ask the jury not only to find the defendant not guilty of murder, but not guilty of manslaughter either. They should try to picture the two parties in the case, and imagine the sort of man the father was, and contrast him with the young man who had stammered out his evidence a short while before. The father was said to be much taller and stronger than his son, and he had a bad temper. He was a man who had driven his wife from home, thereby depriving his son of a mother's love and affection.

There had been many rumours about the case. It had been said that a short time before his death, Mr Wells had received £200 compensation following his accident, but it was entirely untrue. When arrested the boy had not a penny on him, and there was only a farthing in the house when the police searched it. 'We have a squalid home and the father was a slaughter man,' Mr Cotes-Preedy said. His boy had helped him from the age of nine, which explained why he was not more disturbed by the sight of blood. The allegation of the prosecution that Mr Wells had been struck from behind while sitting down rested solely on the evidence of Dr Washbourn, and he had not expressed a definite opinion on the point. In conclusion, the counsel for the defence asked the jury to believe Ronald's story – that he had not meant to kill his father.

Summing up the case, Judge Hawke said that the prosecution had not suggested for one moment that this was a premeditated murder. If the members of the jury were satisfied that the death of George Wells was the result of provocation which no reasonable man could withstand, then they were entitled to bring in a verdict of manslaughter. If they thought the blows were necessary for self-defence, and Ronald Wells did nothing more than was necessary to defend himself, then they could find him not guilty.

The jury retired to consider their verdict, returning to court after an absence of thirty-five minutes. Ronald Wells was brought into the dock and the foreman of the jury announced that they found the defendant not guilty of murder. At this, applause broke out from some women in the gallery, which was quickly suppressed by the judge. The jury foreman then said that they found Wells guilty of manslaughter. The judge said he would deliver his sentence after lunch.

When the judge resumed his seat after the break, Detective Sergeant Ward gave evidence regarding Wells's character, and revealed his previous criminal record. Although he had a history of theft, there had been no violence involved in any of his crimes.

The judge then addressed Ronald Wells, telling him, 'I am afraid I must pass a severe sentence upon you, Wells, but because you are comparatively young it will be less than it otherwise would have been.' He added that Wells had done a very wicked thing, and that lack of self-control was not a defence to committing crime. 'The sentence which I pass on you is that you

Front page of *The Citizen*, 30 January 1935. (Gloucestershire Archives)

111

will be kept in penal servitude for five years.' Ronald Wells was hurried from the dock by two warders.

In June 1939, a convict out on licence appeared before the Bench at the Somerset Quarter Sessions in Taunton, charged with stealing £20 from his stepbrother, with whom he had been living at Compton Durville, near Yeovil. Ronald George Wells, aged twenty-four, said he had taken the money in order to go and join the army, with the intention of concealing the fact that he was a convict on licence. He had taken the £20 off a roll of notes containing £50 in total. He had been arrested in Birmingham, having already joined up.

The court was told that Wells had been employed by Captain Firth at Compton Abdale as a general labourer and stable hand for about five months. Firth had found Wells to be honest and hardworking. The accused was single and a native of Taunton; his family had moved to Gloucester when he was a baby.

The magistrates said they were inclined to give Wells another chance. He would have to serve the unexpired period of penal servitude, and on release he would be placed on probation for three years. Ronald Wells was taken back to prison.

Lightning Source UK Ltd.
Milton Keynes UK
UKOW03f1705260713

214447UK00003B/110/P